3 9082 03373291 1

D1503651

SOUTHGATE VETERANS MEMORIAL LIBRARY

CONSTANTINE

CONSTANTINE

Nancy Zinsser Walworth

CHELSEA HOUSE PUBLISHERS
NEW YORK
PHILADELPHIA

Chelsea House Publishers

EDITOR-IN-CHIEF: Nancy Toff
EXECUTIVE EDITOR: Remmel T. Nunn
MANAGING EDITOR: Karyn Gullen Browne
COPY CHIEF: Juliann Barbato
PICTURE EDITOR: Adrian G. Allen
ART DIRECTOR: Maria Epes
MANUFACTURING MANAGER: Gerald Levine

World Leaders—Past & Present

SENIOR EDITOR: John W. Selfridge

Staff for CONSTANTINE

ASSISTANT EDITOR: Terrance Dolan
DEPUTY COPY CHIEF: Nicole Bowen
EDITORIAL ASSISTANT: Nate Eaton
PICTURE RESEARCHER: Alan Gottlieb
ASSISTANT ART DIRECTOR: Loraine Machlin
DESIGNER: David Murray
DESIGN ASSISTANT: James Baker
PRODUCTION COORDINATOR: Joseph Romano
COVER ILLUSTRATION: Robert Caputo

First Printing

1 3 5 7 9 8 6 4 2

Library of Congress Cataloging-in-Publication Data

Walworth, Nancy Zinsser.
    Constantine.
    p.   cm.—(World leaders past & present)
    Bibliography: p.
    Includes index.
    Summary: A biography of Constantine the Great, who was the
first emperor of Rome to become a Christian, and who made
Constantinople (now Istanbul, Turkey) the capital of his empire, a
move some historians consider the beginnings of Byzantine
history.
ISBN 1-55546-805-5
        0-7910-0692-1 (pbk.)
    1. Constantine I, Emperor of Rome, d. 337—Juvenile literature.
2. Roman emperors—Biography—Juvenile literature. 3. Rome—
History—Constantine I, the Great, 306–337—Juvenile literature.
[1. Constantine I, Emperor of Rome, d. 337. 2. Kings, queens,
rulers, etc.] I. Title. II. Series.
DG315.W29   1989   89–33128
937'.08'092—dc20
[B]   CIP
[92]   AC

Contents

- JOHN ADAMS
- JOHN QUINCY ADAMS
- KONRAD ADENAUER
- ALEXANDER THE GREAT
- SALVADOR ALLENDE
- MARC ANTONY
- CORAZON AQUINO
- YASIR ARAFAT
- KING ARTHUR
- HAFEZ AL-ASSAD
- KEMAL ATATÜRK
- ATTILA
- CLEMENT ATTLEE
- AUGUSTUS CAESAR
- MENACHEM BEGIN
- DAVID BEN-GURION
- OTTO VON BISMARCK
- LÉON BLUM
- SIMON BOLÍVAR
- CESARE BORGIA
- WILLY BRANDT
- LEONID BREZHNEV
- JULIUS CAESAR
- JOHN CALVIN
- JIMMY CARTER
- FIDEL CASTRO
- CATHERINE THE GREAT
- CHARLEMAGNE
- CHIANG KAI-SHEK
- WINSTON CHURCHILL
- GEORGES CLEMENCEAU
- CLEOPATRA
- CONSTANTINE THE GREAT
- HERNÁN CORTÉS
- OLIVER CROMWELL
- GEORGES-JACQUES DANTON
- JEFFERSON DAVIS
- MOSHE DAYAN
- CHARLES DE GAULLE
- EAMON DE VALERA
- EUGENE DEBS
- DENG XIAOPING
- BENJAMIN DISRAELI
- ALEXANDER DUBČEK
- FRANÇOIS & JEAN-CLAUDE DUVALIER
- DWIGHT EISENHOWER
- ELEANOR OF AQUITAINE
- ELIZABETH I
- FAISAL
- FERDINAND & ISABELLA
- FRANCISCO FRANCO
- BENJAMIN FRANKLIN
- FREDERICK THE GREAT
- INDIRA GANDHI
- MOHANDAS GANDHI
- GIUSEPPE GARIBALDI
- AMIN & BASHIR GEMAYEL
- GENGHIS KHAN
- WILLIAM GLADSTONE
- MIKHAIL GORBACHEV
- ULYSSES S. GRANT
- ERNESTO "CHE" GUEVARA
- TENZIN GYATSO
- ALEXANDER HAMILTON
- DAG HAMMARSKJÖLD
- HENRY VIII
- HENRY OF NAVARRE
- PAUL VON HINDENBURG
- HIROHITO
- ADOLF HITLER
- HO CHI MINH
- KING HUSSEIN
- IVAN THE TERRIBLE
- ANDREW JACKSON
- JAMES I
- WOJCIECH JARUZELSKI
- THOMAS JEFFERSON
- JOAN OF ARC
- POPE JOHN XXIII
- POPE JOHN PAUL II
- LYNDON JOHNSON
- BENITO JUÁREZ
- JOHN KENNEDY
- ROBERT KENNEDY
- JOMO KENYATTA
- AYATOLLAH KHOMEINI
- NIKITA KHRUSHCHEV
- KIM IL SUNG
- MARTIN LUTHER KING, JR.
- HENRY KISSINGER
- KUBLAI KHAN
- LAFAYETTE
- ROBERT E. LEE
- VLADIMIR LENIN
- ABRAHAM LINCOLN
- DAVID LLOYD GEORGE
- LOUIS XIV
- MARTIN LUTHER
- JUDAS MACCABEUS
- JAMES MADISON
- NELSON & WINNIE MANDELA
- MAO ZEDONG
- FERDINAND MARCOS
- GEORGE MARSHALL
- MARY, QUEEN OF SCOTS
- TOMÁŠ MASARYK
- GOLDA MEIR
- KLEMENS VON METTERNICH
- JAMES MONROE
- HOSNI MUBARAK
- ROBERT MUGABE
- BENITO MUSSOLINI
- NAPOLÉON BONAPARTE
- GAMAL ABDEL NASSER
- JAWAHARLAL NEHRU
- NERO
- NICHOLAS II
- RICHARD NIXON
- KWAME NKRUMAH
- DANIEL ORTEGA
- MOHAMMED REZA PAHLAVI
- THOMAS PAINE
- CHARLES STEWART PARNELL
- PERICLES
- JUAN PERÓN
- PETER THE GREAT
- POL POT
- MUAMMAR EL-QADDAFI
- RONALD REAGAN
- CARDINAL RICHELIEU
- MAXIMILIEN ROBESPIERRE
- ELEANOR ROOSEVELT
- FRANKLIN ROOSEVELT
- THEODORE ROOSEVELT
- ANWAR SADAT
- HAILE SELASSIE
- PRINCE SIHANOUK
- JAN SMUTS
- JOSEPH STALIN
- SUKARNO
- SUN YAT-SEN
- TAMERLANE
- MOTHER TERESA
- MARGARET THATCHER
- JOSIP BROZ TITO
- TOUSSAINT L'OUVERTURE
- LEON TROTSKY
- PIERRE TRUDEAU
- HARRY TRUMAN
- QUEEN VICTORIA
- LECH WALESA
- GEORGE WASHINGTON
- CHAIM WEIZMANN
- WOODROW WILSON
- XERXES
- EMILIANO ZAPATA
- ZHOU ENLAI

CHELSEA HOUSE PUBLISHERS

ON LEADERSHIP

Arthur M. Schlesinger, jr.

LEADERSHIP, it may be said, is really what makes the world go round. Love no doubt smooths the passage; but love is a private transaction between consenting adults. Leadership is a public transaction with history. The idea of leadership affirms the capacity of individuals to move, inspire, and mobilize masses of people so that they act together in pursuit of an end. Sometimes leadership serves good purposes, sometimes bad; but whether the end is benign or evil, great leaders are those men and women who leave their personal stamp on history.

Now, the very concept of leadership implies the proposition that individuals can make a difference. This proposition has never been universally accepted. From classical times to the present day, eminent thinkers have regarded individuals as no more than the agents and pawns of larger forces, whether the gods and goddesses of the ancient world or, in the modern era, race, class, nation, the dialectic, the will of the people, the spirit of the times, history itself. Against such forces, the individual dwindles into insignificance.

So contends the thesis of historical determinism. Tolstoy's great novel *War and Peace* offers a famous statement of the case. Why, Tolstoy asked, did millions of men in the Napoleonic Wars, denying their human feelings and their common sense, move back and forth across Europe slaughtering their fellows? "The war," Tolstoy answered, "was bound to happen simply because it was bound to happen." All prior history predetermined it. As for leaders, they, Tolstoy said, "are but the labels that serve to give a name to an end and, like labels, they have the least possible connection with the event." The greater the leader, "the more conspicuous the inevitability and the predestination of every act he commits." The leader, said Tolstoy, is "the slave of history."

Determinism takes many forms. Marxism is the determinism of class. Nazism the determinism of race. But the idea of men and women as the slaves of history runs athwart the deepest human instincts. Rigid determinism abolishes the idea of human freedom—

the assumption of free choice that underlies every move we make, every word we speak, every thought we think. It abolishes the idea of human responsibility, since it is manifestly unfair to reward or punish people for actions that are by definition beyond their control. No one can live consistently by any deterministic creed. The Marxist states prove this themselves by their extreme susceptibility to the cult of leadership.

More than that, history refutes the idea that individuals make no difference. In December 1931 a British politician crossing Park Avenue in New York City between 76th and 77th Streets around 10:30 P.M. looked in the wrong direction and was knocked down by an automobile—a moment, he later recalled, of a man aghast, a world aglare: "I do not understand why I was not broken like an eggshell or squashed like a gooseberry." Fourteen months later an American politician, sitting in an open car in Miami, Florida, was fired on by an assassin; the man beside him was hit. Those who believe that individuals make no difference to history might well ponder whether the next two decades would have been the same had Mario Constasino's car killed Winston Churchill in 1931 and Giuseppe Zangara's bullet killed Franklin Roosevelt in 1933. Suppose, in addition, that Adolf Hitler had been killed in the street fighting during the Munich *Putsch* of 1923 and that Lenin had died of typhus during World War I. What would the 20th century be like now?

For better or for worse, individuals do make a difference. "The notion that a people can run itself and its affairs anonymously," wrote the philosopher William James, "is now well known to be the silliest of absurdities. Mankind does nothing save through initiatives on the part of inventors, great or small, and imitation by the rest of us—these are the sole factors in human progress. Individuals of genius show the way, and set the patterns, which common people then adopt and follow."

Leadership, James suggests, means leadership in thought as well as in action. In the long run, leaders in thought may well make the greater difference to the world. But, as Woodrow Wilson once said, "Those only are leaders of men, in the general eye, who lead in action. . . . It is at their hands that new thought gets its translation into the crude language of deeds." Leaders in thought often invent in solitude and obscurity, leaving to later generations the tasks of imitation. Leaders in action—the leaders portrayed in this series—have to be effective in their own time.

And they cannot be effective by themselves. They must act in response to the rhythms of their age. Their genius must be adapted, in a phrase of William James's, "to the receptivities of the moment." Leaders are useless without followers. "There goes the mob," said the French politician hearing a clamor in the streets. "I am their leader. I must follow them." Great leaders turn the inchoate emotions of the mob to purposes of their own. They seize on the opportunities of their time, the hopes, fears, frustrations, crises, potentialities. They succeed when events have prepared the way for them, when the community is awaiting to be aroused, when they can provide the clarifying and organizing ideas. Leadership ignites the circuit between the individual and the mass and thereby alters history.

It may alter history for better or for worse. Leaders have been responsible for the most extravagant follies and most monstrous crimes that have beset suffering humanity. They have also been vital in such gains as humanity has made in individual freedom, religious and racial tolerance, social justice, and respect for human rights.

There is no sure way to tell in advance who is going to lead for good and who for evil. But a glance at the gallery of men and women in *World Leaders—Past and Present* suggests some useful tests.

One test is this: Do leaders lead by force or by persuasion? By command or by consent? Through most of history leadership was exercised by the divine right of authority. The duty of followers was to defer and to obey. "Theirs not to reason why / Theirs but to do and die." On occasion, as with the so-called enlightened despots of the 18th century in Europe, absolutist leadership was animated by humane purposes. More often, absolutism nourished the passion for domination, land, gold, and conquest and resulted in tyranny.

The great revolution of modern times has been the revolution of equality. The idea that all people should be equal in their legal condition has undermined the old structure of authority, hierarchy, and deference. The revolution of equality has had two contrary effects on the nature of leadership. For equality, as Alexis de Tocqueville pointed out in his great study *Democracy in America,* might mean equality in servitude as well as equality in freedom.

"I know of only two methods of establishing equality in the political world," Tocqueville wrote. "Rights must be given to every citizen, or none at all to anyone . . . save one, who is the master of all." There was no middle ground "between the sovereignty of all and the absolute power of one man." In his astonishing prediction of 20th-century totalitarian dictatorship, Tocqueville explained how the revolution of equality could lead to the *"Führerprinzip"* and more terrible absolutism than the world had ever known.

But when rights are given to every citizen and the sovereignty of all is established, the problem of leadership takes a new form, becomes more exacting than ever before. It is easy to issue commands and enforce them by the rope and the stake, the concentration camp and the *gulag.* It is much harder to use argument and achievement to overcome opposition and win consent. The Founding Fathers of the United States understood the difficulty. They believed that history had given them the opportunity to decide, as Alexander Hamilton wrote in the first Federalist Paper, whether men are indeed capable of basing government on "reflection and choice, or whether they are forever destined to depend . . . on accident and force."

Government by reflection and choice called for a new style of leadership and a new quality of followership. It required leaders to be responsive to popular concerns, and it required followers to be active and informed participants in the process. Democracy does not eliminate emotion from politics; sometimes it fosters demagoguery; but it is confident that, as the greatest of democratic leaders put it, you cannot fool all of the people all of the time. It measures leadership by results and retires those who overreach or falter or fail.

It is true that in the long run despots are measured by results too. But they can postpone the day of judgment, sometimes indefinitely, and in the meantime they can do infinite harm. It is also true that democracy is no guarantee of virtue and intelligence in government, for the voice of the people is not necessarily the voice of God. But democracy, by assuring the right of opposition, offers built-in resistance to the evils inherent in absolutism. As the theologian Reinhold Niebuhr summed it up, "Man's capacity for justice makes democracy possible, but man's inclination to injustice makes democracy necessary."

A second test for leadership is the end for which power is sought. When leaders have as their goal the supremacy of a master race or the promotion of totalitarian revolution or the acquisition and exploitation of colonies or the protection of greed and privilege or the preservation of personal power, it is likely that their leadership will do little to advance the cause of humanity. When their goal is the abolition of slavery, the liberation of women, the enlargement of opportunity for the poor and powerless, the extension of equal rights to racial minorities, the defense of the freedoms of expression and opposition, it is likely that their leadership will increase the sum of human liberty and welfare.

Leaders have done great harm to the world. They have also conferred great benefits. You will find both sorts in this series. Even "good" leaders must be regarded with a certain wariness. Leaders are not demigods; they put on their trousers one leg after another just like ordinary mortals. No leader is infallible, and every leader needs to be reminded of this at regular intervals. Irreverence irritates leaders but is their salvation. Unquestioning submission corrupts leaders and demeans followers. Making a cult of a leader is always a mistake. Fortunately hero worship generates its own antidote. "Every hero," said Emerson, "becomes a bore at last."

The signal benefit the great leaders confer is to embolden the rest of us to live according to our own best selves, to be active, insistent, and resolute in affirming our own sense of things. For great leaders attest to the reality of human freedom against the supposed inevitabilities of history. And they attest to the wisdom and power that may lie within the most unlikely of us, which is why Abraham Lincoln remains the supreme example of great leadership. A great leader, said Emerson, exhibits new possibilities to all humanity. "We feed on genius. . . . Great men exist that there may be greater men."

Great leaders, in short, justify themselves by emancipating and empowering their followers. So humanity struggles to master its destiny, remembering with Alexis de Tocqueville: "It is true that around every man a fatal circle is traced beyond which he cannot pass; but within the wide verge of that circle he is powerful and free; as it is with man, so with communities."

ADLOCVTIO
QVADIVINI
TVS IMPVLSV
CONSTANTIN
ANI VICTORIAM
REPERERI

1

An Extraordinary Dream

The great Flaminian road that led to Rome was dusty under the boots of Constantine's legions as they advanced on the city in the autumn of A.D. 312. Though Constantine, a young Roman general, had declared himself Roman emperor of the west, another Roman, Maxentius, occupied the city and also claimed to be emperor. Constantine was intent on settling the matter once and for all. He and Maxentius had each been proclaimed emperor by their own troops, and both men were well prepared for the coming confrontation.

Wearing helmets and heavy body armor, Constantine's troops and cavalrymen sweated as they marched under the hot sun. They were northern men, used to the brisk October winds of Britain, upper Gaul (modern France), and the German frontier. The countryside through which they marched was far more cultivated and civilized than the wild, forested lands from which most of them had come.

Italian Renaissance painter Raphael's interpretation of Constantine's fateful dream, in which the warring Roman emperor claimed to have seen and received counsel from Jesus Christ. Constantine's mystical experience marked a turning point in European history as Christianity emerged as the dominant religion in the Western world.

The Appian Way, built from the 4th to the 2nd century B.C. and leading from Rome to the Adriatic port of Brindisi 350 miles away, is the oldest of the great Roman roads. The spine of the empire's highway system, the Romans called it the *regina viarum*, the "queen of roads."

As they approached the outskirts of the ancient capital city, the scenery changed from harvested fields and bare vineyards to a series of manicured gardens surrounding opulent red-roofed mansions. Along the roadside were the ornate ancestral mausoleums of the rich and the humbler cemeteries of the poor. Mixed in among these were shrines to local pagan gods — mostly unfamiliar to the marchers, who worshiped other deities. Gradually, taverns and small shops could be seen along the roadway, but they were boarded up and deserted by their owners, who had heard rumors of the arriving army. The ordinary traffic of this important trunk route had slowed except for peasants who scurried off at the sight of the invaders. Remembering other civil wars that had ravaged their beautiful countryside, they hurried to hide their familes and livestock while there was still time.

14

When Constantine's scouts returned from a careful look at the enemy's situation, they reported that the city seemed impregnable. Its enormous walls, built by the emperor Aurelian 30 years earlier, had been strengthened and heightened by Maxentius. New towers at intervals along the walls were manned by artillery men in charge of rock-hurling machines. The scouts also reported that many barges, in preparation for a siege, were unloading grain at the city's docks along the Tiber River. The river would have to be crossed by Constantine's troops over the arched and narrow Milvian Bridge, although the scouts reported that next to it was a new temporary bridge of planking supported by boats.

The Aurelian Wall of Rome, built by the emperor Aurelian in A.D. 282 and reinforced by Maxentius 30 years later, presented a daunting obstacle to the forces of Constantine as they approached the city on October 27, A.D. 312.

The Milvian Bridge, spanning the Tiber River where it passes close to Rome, was the focal point of the fierce battle for control of the great city between the forces of Constantine and those of Maxentius.

Constantine concealed his feelings at this forbidding information, brought his troops to a halt, and ordered his men to pitch camp for the night. They were about eight miles from Rome. He wanted his men to eat, relax, and rest well in preparation for their attack on Rome the next morning. He held a conference with his staff, giving them orders for the following day, and retired to his tent. He probably prayed to the sun-god, giver of light — the favorite god of the legions — to grant him victory. He felt uncertain and nervous, worrying that he had perhaps made a foolhardy gamble on his future.

Finally, Constantine fell into a restless sleep. Sometime during the night he had an extraordinary dream in which he received a visit from Jesus Christ, the god of the new Christian sect that was spreading through the Roman Empire. During this visit, Constantine was commanded to paint Christ's initials on the shields of his soldiers and was promised that under the protection of these holy letters he would be victorious.

This inspiring vision and command changed Constantine's life. He awoke convinced that the Christian god was all-powerful and that his command must be obeyed. At dawn he ordered his armorers to paint Christ's initials on his helmet and on as many shields as possible. Then, under the protection of the emblem, the army advanced on Rome.

Constantine's victory on October 28, A.D. 312 over an enemy protected by ancient gods persuaded him to become a Christian. That crucial victory led him on to other victories under the Christian banner. When he finally became Rome's undisputed emperor, he used his wealth and power to advance the growth of the Christian church and to weaken pagan worship throughout his vast empire. After his death the Christians continued to expand and eventually change the face of the world.

Flavius Valerius Constantinus, the first Christian Roman emperor, also known as Constantine the Great, was born on February 27 in the closing years of the third century A.D. The year of his birth is unknown. Some scholars say that he was born in 284 and had his famous dream and won his crucial battle while still in his twenties. Other scholars, consulting other sources, say that he was born 5 or 10 years earlier. The place where Constantine was born is also disputed. Three different birthplaces have been suggested — one in England, one in Asia Minor, and the third in Yugoslavia.

There are no hard facts to prove or disprove any of these theories, for Constantine and his contemporaries neglected to record much of his personal life. Most of his modern biographers, after weighing ancient, conflicting evidence, have concluded that the place of his birth was the town of Naissus in the Roman province of Illyria (the modern town of Niš, Yugoslavia) and that the date of his birth was about A.D. 280.

The Age of Constantine is strangely obscure. Most of the hard facts, confidently given in encyclopedias, soften or dissolve upon examination.
—EVELYN WAUGH
English novelist

This likeness of Constantius Chlorus, Constantine's father, can be seen in the Arch of Constantine in Rome. The elaborate triumphal arch was commissioned by the senators of Rome in honor of Constantine's defeat of Maxentius.

Constantius, the father of Constantine, started life as a peasant's son in Illyria's harsh and rugged interior, not too far from one of the worst pressure points on the empire's endangered frontier. Illyria had long been an excellent recruiting ground for the soldiers and officers of the Roman army. Since joining the army was the best way for ambitious peasant boys to get ahead in the Roman world, Constantius followed the local pattern and joined up as soon as he was eligible. His comrades gave him the Latin nickname Chlorus, or "Pale One." His pallor might have been caused by the tight control he kept on his emotions, for he was an intense, driven man of great ability who had to cope throughout his life with stress and danger.

Chlorus lived in a time when the Roman Empire was going through dark days, a time of anarchy and despair. By the middle of the third century the empire's thousands of miles of frontier were being overrun at many points by barbarian tribes. Roman emperors, once men of broad experience and enlightened government, were now mostly rough army officers with little education. A strong leader was desperately needed, but in the years when young Chlorus was working his way up from the bottom ranks of the army, the few emperors who showed real ability were assassinated after brief reigns.

It had not always been this way. The Roman Empire had been created 250 years before by the young Augustus Caesar, who in 27 B.C. took the collapsing Roman Republic into his own hands and transformed it into a state run by one man — the emperor.

A statue of Augustus Caesar belonging to the Vatican Museum in Rome. Augustus was the first of a long line of powerful Roman emperors. By Constantine's time, however, the empire had begun to fail.

A brilliant and shrewd ruler, he disguised his power by continuing the former constitutional system of popular elections of officials and senators, thus pleasing both the people and the powerful upper classes. Under his supervision the laws and traditions of ancient Rome were upheld. The invigorated empire expanded in influence and territory. By the time of Augustus's death, the boundaries of the empire extended over an enormous area around the Mediterranean Sea — bounded in the north and west by ocean and channel, to the east by three great rivers (the Rhine, the Danube, and the Euphrates), and to the south by the fearsome deserts on the borders of its African and Arabian provinces. Beyond these varied frontiers were barbarian tribes, constantly threatening, constantly on the march, but always held back by the disciplined and highly mobile legions of the Roman army.

Many remarkable emperors succeeded Augustus

A painting of the Forum, the civic center of ancient Rome. Built in a low-lying area between four hills, the Forum was the place where commerce, social interaction, and political debate and administration all took place. Many of the most dramatic events in Roman history occurred in the Forum.

in the first two centuries A.D. Their ancient capital, Rome, the seat of their power, grew in importance and splendor. Situated on seven hills, it became a city of gleaming pagan temples and immense imperial palaces and government buildings, intermixed with massive public works — baths, stadiums, monuments, markets, and parks — for the people. Long lines of aqueducts reached out in all directions from the city's seven hills. Excellent roads radiated from Rome's Golden Milestone to the farthest corners of the empire, a superb communications system for trade and speedy defense. At Rome's nearby port, Ostia, at the mouth of the Tiber River, there was a steady stream of shipping, protected by the war galleys of the Roman navy. Roman merchants traded with chieftains from Scandinavia to Ethiopia, even sending — by the middle of the second century — more than a hundred ships a year to India and a few to China.

A stone relief portrays a helmeted Roman soldier battling a long-haired barbarian. At the time of Constantine's birth, late in the 3rd century A.D., barbarian tribes were beginning to overrun the perimeter of the Roman territory.

For almost two centuries the many races and nations within the protected and well-governed Roman world enjoyed prosperity and a deep peace, the *Pax Romana*, or Roman peace, that is celebrated in history. Romans believed that this golden age would last forever, but in A.D. 180, with the degenerate emperor Commodus, Rome's luck began to change.

Within a century the Roman Empire fell to the lowest point in its long history, just when Constantius Chlorus, the father of Constantine the Great, joined the army, earned his first promotions, and was given small border commands on the dangerous Danube River frontier. Border tribes were attacking all over the empire, and frontiers were collapsing. In A.D. 260 large bands of horsemen from Persia (modern Iran) conquered the important Roman provinces of Mesopotamia and Syria, seriously threatening the empire's rich eastern trade and — most shocking of all — capturing the Roman emperor Valerian. This unfortunate emperor, representing in his person the invulnerable might of Rome, was the only Roman ruler in its thousand-year history to fall into the hands of an enemy.

Three thousand miles away, at the empire's northernmost point in Britain, Picts, a wild people constantly involved in border wars with the Romans, were breaking through Hadrian's defensive wall. At the empire's southern extremity, desert tribes, using camels militarily for the first time, were raiding the rich province of Egypt. German tribes even crossed the Alps into the Italian motherland itself, and although the emperor Aurelian forced them to retreat, he took the precaution of heightening the walls of mighty Rome itself, some 300 miles to the south.

An outbreak of the plague, brought back by Roman soldiers from the Persian Wars, spread through the Roman east, raging for 15 years and leaving whole districts and towns empty and thus ripe for further invasions. A devastating earthquake added

The defeated Roman emperor Valerian kneels before victorious King Shapur of Persia following the battle of Edessa, in A.D. 260. Valerian was taken prisoner by the Persians and never seen again.

to the squalor and desolation. Taking advantage of weakness and disorder, some ambitious army generals who promised higher pay and booty to their troops were in return proclaimed emperors, thus producing the unsettling situation of two or more Roman emperors competing for power. Their reigns were short, but their violent ways caused great damage to the unity of the state. Thoughtful citizens, trying to cope with exhausted resources and worthless money, foresaw the impossible — the end of the Roman Empire.

The rising young Roman officer Constantius Chlorus spent these years commanding troops in the frontier areas of his native Illyria, where German tribes constantly probed for Roman weakness. It was probably early in his army career that he first met Helena, the woman who was to become Constantine's mother and a famous Christian saint.

There are many legends about Helena's origins — the most appealing one (and the least probable) is that she was the redheaded daughter of the Celtic king Coel of Britain and that the pale, reserved Roman officer met her on a secret military mission for the emperor. A more likely traditional account is that Chlorus, off duty one day in the river town of Naissus, entered a popular local tavern, met the tavern keeper's young daughter Helena and fell in love. Though Helena's later political enemies whispered that she had been a prostitute and that her son, Constantine, was illegitimate, it is probable that they were legally married.

Constantine was their only child, much loved by both parents all their lives in spite of the later dissolution of their marriage and their long separations from him. He was a blond, blue-eyed, and sturdy baby with a pleasing manner. He and his mother, like a typical army family today, must have been stationed at many posts, often waiting long periods for Chlorus's return from duty. They must have also moved with him when, according to one old source, he was made governor of Dalmatia, a beautiful coastal part of Illyria with a temperate climate. The governorship was a huge step up politically for a man who had started at the bottom.

A Roman coin bearing the image of Helena, the mother of Constantine. Helena was unceremoniously abandoned by her husband, Constantius Chlorus, for political reasons. Upon becoming emperor many years later, however, Constantine elevated her to a position of queenly status.

Diocletian rose through the ranks of the Roman army to become the greatest of the Illyrian soldier-emperors of the 3rd century. As emperor, he instituted a series of military and administrative reforms that revived the flagging empire.

When Constantine was about four years old, the emperor Numerian, returning from an expedition to Persia, kept the curtains of his litter closed to protect his inflamed eyes from the bright eastern sun. His scheming father-in-law stabbed him to death while his litter was unattended. His porters, unaware of the murder, picked up the litter and carried the curtained body on its way. Meanwhile, the murderer sent messages ahead to the coemperor Carinus in Rome.

But after a few days someone discovered the dead emperor within the litter. The troops, enraged at the deed, held a council of war and, disliking the other emperor in Rome, proclaimed their popular commander, Valerius Diocles, emperor. This soldier, known to history as Diocletian, turned out to be very different from his predecessors. During his extraordinary 20-year rule, he arrested the downhill slide of the Roman world and created a climate of change in which young Constantine would thrive.

2

The Young Patrician

The news of the murder of the emperor Numerian and the elevation of Diocletian traveled swiftly along the fast trunk road from the city of Nicomedia in Asia Minor to the army camp in Illyria, where Chlorus, his wife, Helena, and their four-year-old son, Constantine, were stationed. Chlorus must have hoped that the new emperor would take notice of him and advance his career, for Diocletian happened to be an Illyrian of the same humble origins and with the same honest, trustworthy character.

Before Diocletian could make new appointments, he had to dispose of the other emperor in Rome — which he did in battle within the year. He was now the sole ruler of the huge and chaotic Roman Empire. Within six months he decided that reorganizing and running the empire was too difficult for one man. In the fall of A.D. 286 he appointed as co-emperor an Illyrian general named Maximian (Marcus Aurelius Valerius Maximianus), who had fought

Diocletian made three partners of his realm, dividing the empire into four parts and multiplying the armies, while each of them aspired to have a far larger number than earlier emperors had when they governed alone.
—LACTANTIUS
4th-century rhetorician

In A.D. 287 this gold medallion was issued to Roman officers of the higher ranks. The front of the coin bears the images of the coemperors Diocletian (left) and Maximian. The reverse side shows a consular procession complete with elephants and palm-waving crowds.

well in the Persian Wars and who, though uneducated and brutal, could be counted on to serve loyally. Diocletian, while making it clear to Maximian that he, Diocletian, would retain the dominant role in Roman affairs, turned over to him the management of the western half of the empire.

Then Chlorus got his promotion. He became Maximian's praetorian prefect, or chief military assistant, with the important command of the Roman armies in Gaul.

Constantine was six years old at the time of his father's promotion. He and his parents said good-bye to their native country and, with a staff befitting their new rank, headed out toward Chlorus's future headquarters, close to the north German border. His father, impressive in his splendid new military uniform, rode a fine army mount and let Constantine ride on a pony by his side. Helena and her attendants accompanied them in four-wheeled curtained carriages. A large retinue of slaves, attendants, secretaries, and special army units made up the rest of the party. They rode for many days on good Roman roads that curved around the sides of mountains, crossed streams, and cut through valleys and over high mountain passes. They changed horses and received and sent dispatches at regular imperial posts. Quartermasters arranged for supplies along the way, paying for them out of the bottomless imperial purse.

Finally, the group approached the strategic fortress-city of Trier, situated in the fertile grain- and wine-growing valley of the Moselle River, a tributary of the Rhine. It was Constantine's first experience in a big Roman fortified city. Looking across the river from a distant hill, he saw huge wharves and warehouses and, behind them, high turreted walls that enclosed even higher roofs and towers. His father assured him that the city was impregnable, for attackers would have to cross the city's two lines of moats and then survive a rain of catapulted boulders before they could even reach the city's well-defended walls. The party crossed the stone bridge that arched across the river and rode through the immense gateway into the city. Legions of Chlorus's

The life of Saint Helena begins and ends in surmise and legend.
—EVELYN WAUGH
English novelist

new command lined up in formation along the way, and curious crowds pushed to get a look at their new commander and his handsome six-year-old son riding proudly by his side.

The family settled down to a much grander life than they had known before. Everyone deferred to the prefect, whose authority in the region was supreme, and praised his young son.

Constantine often accompanied his father when he relaxed at the public baths after a morning of hard work. Everyone bathed even on the coldest winter days in this northern city, for the marbled walls and floors of the great covered bathing halls were heated by immense areas of furnaces and steam pipes. First they would choose one of three warm pools, all in a single room. Then, wrapped in towels, they would move to the middle hall and slide into a cooler pool, followed by a quick plunge into one of five very cold pools in the huge *frigidarium*.

In autumn A.D. 286, Chlorus and his six-year-old son Constantine rode through the gateway of the heavily fortified city of Trier, in Gaul. Young Constantine was awed by the massive fortress.

The ruins of Diocletian's baths in Rome. The Romans brought the luxurious trappings of their capital city to even the most isolated outposts of the empire. Chlorus and his family were pleasantly surprised to find Roman baths at the frontier city of Trier.

After this would come the sweat rooms, massage rooms, and dressing rooms, all decorated with mosaics and statuary. On leaving, father and son would walk through colonnades to the outside athletic field. Here men would often take time off from their exercising to instruct their commander's son in various sports, including the proper use of sword and dagger.

On special days the family would go to the amphitheater in the middle of the city, where they would sit in a special section reserved for persons of rank and watch various spectacles, such as throwing criminals or German prisoners to hungry lions and wolves.

On other days, Chlorus would take leave of his family to worship in the great sanctuary of the sun-god Mithras, a god that Roman soldiers had learned of in the Near East. A religion for men only, Mithraism promised victory and life after death for its followers. Chlorus had been initiated into this cult as a young soldier. In order to join it, he had undergone such terrifying initiation rites as being singed by fire or thrown, hands together, across a deep pit before he was given the final purifying bath in the blood of a slaughtered bull. Constantine was too young to accompany his father to the secret rites of Mithras and to be admitted to his cult, but meanwhile he was taught by his parents to worship ancient Roman gods, along with family ancestral gods, and lesser spirits of the mountains and fields, whose powers were apparent in every flood or thunderstorm.

The temple of the sun-god Mithras in Rome. Mithras was worshiped by men only, and the practice was especially popular among Roman soldiers. Initiates were bathed in the warm blood of a freshly slaughtered bull.

In addition, Helena may have become interested in Christianity and influenced her son in this direction, although he was not aware of the strength of her influence at the time. Christianity was a fairly new religion in the Roman world. Its message was sympathetic to women and the poor, and its teachings were personal — a striking contrast to the dry ceremonial religion of the Roman state. A number of Christians lived in Gaul, and many of them were employed in Trier. Helena may have talked with Christian women and become familiar with at least some of their beliefs. There is no proof that she did, but it is known that sometime during her adult life Helena became a Christian and that her son, Constantine, before his sudden conversion in his early thirties, had been acquainted with much of the drama and promise of Christianity. Because Constantine was alone with his mother so much during Chlorus's many Gallic campaigns, it is entirely possible that during their many hours together she passed on to him some of the stirring Christian Gospel stories. At the time, however, the boy probably preferred his father's god — the sun-god of the soldiers.

In the first two years in Trier, Constantine's father concluded a successful series of campaigns against German tribes that had broken through Roman lines on the frontier and advanced into Gaul. After a tremendous victory in A.D. 268 he was awarded a victory parade, or "triumph," by Diocletian's coemperor Maximian, who came north from his headquarters in Milan in northern Italy to take part in it. It was the first of many triumphs that Constantine was to view: a long procession of returning veterans, terrified prisoners in chains, wagonloads of trophies and booty, and lastly, his father, the triumphant praetorian prefect, riding with Emperor Maximian himself in purple robes and a golden wreath.

The family spent seven years in Gaul. During this time Constantine grew tall and muscular. His jaw grew firm, as if to reflect his iron will and desire to excel. Like most soldiers' sons, he learned to play military games in preparation for later military life and showed early a capacity for leadership. As the

The borders of the empire were protected by fortifications, palisades, forts, ditches and walls . . . so that the entire field of Roman civilization formed one vast enclosure.
—JOSEPH VOGT
Dutch historian

A captured enemy chieftain pleads for mercy before the throne of the Roman emperor. As a young boy, the future emperor Constantine acquired a taste for conquest from his father, Chlorus, who directed a series of successful military campaigns from Trier.

praetorian prefect's son, he grew accustomed to special attention and luxury. He seems to have avoided much schooling or tutoring. Helena, though intelligent and energetic, was not an educated person and would not have insisted on schooling if it interfered with her son's athletic or military pursuits.

In 293 their family harmony was suddenly shattered. Emperor Diocletian, from his imperial headquarters far away in Nicomedia, announced his latest system of government, a four-man rule known as the tetrarchy. Each of the two emperors, Diocletian and Maximian, were to be called augustus, an awesome and ancient title. They were to be assisted by two younger men, each to have the even more ancient title of caesar. Each of the four would rule a quarter of the Roman Empire, with Diocletian holding ultimate authority and power. Diocletian's caesar of the east was to be a soldier named Galerius (Galerius Valerius Maximianus) and Constantine's father, Chlorus, was to be caesar of the west. Both Chlorus and Galerius were excellent generals, and that is what mattered most to Emperor Diocletian at that time.

But Chlorus had to accept two conditions if he wanted to be a caesar. The first condition was to divorce Helena, whose origins were considered unsuitable for the wife of the new caesar of the west, and to marry Theodora, the more socially acceptable adopted daughter of the emperor Maximian. Whatever his feelings, Chlorus did not refuse. Helena was abruptly divorced, and his wedding to Theodora followed with great pomp.

Chlorus's second obligation was to send his 13-year-old son, Constantine, halfway across the empire to Diocletian's court in Nicomedia, ostensibly for a better education than he had received at the frontier, but really to be kept as a hostage to ensure his father's loyalty in his powerful new job.

A Roman schoolmaster and his students. Although an academic education was available to the young Constantine, he eschewed it in favor of athletic and military training.

A porphyry statue in San Marco, Venice, represents the tetrarchy of the two caesars, Galerius and Chlorus, and the two augusti, Diocletian and Maximian. Constantine's life changed dramatically when his father was appointed caesar.

Constantine had to say good-bye to his mother without knowing whether he would ever see her again. She was sent away, probably to family or friends back in her native land of Illyria. Her ex-husband, Chlorus, must have seen to it that she would have enough money and that no harm would come to her. She could not have been cut off entirely from her son during the following 30 years, because at the end of that time she suddenly reappeared in history standing by his side as empress dowager.

And Constantine was not to see his father again for 12 years. By that time the pale, intense Chlorus would be dying, and Constantine would be a different person — no longer a boy, but a hardened soldier and calculating politician.

3

Matched by None

The 13-year-old Constantine joined Emperor Diocletian at a military base on the Danube frontier, meeting for the first time the man who was to have such an influence on his career. He saw a vigorous man with short, rough hair and an honest face — but not the face of a man with whom you would want to disagree. Diocletian, a good judge of men, saw a tall, fit adolescent, obviously not very cultured or educated but worth grooming for the future.

From their rendezvous in the winter of 292 they moved south to the emperor's favorite residence in Nicomedia in Asia Minor, pausing on the way at the old city of Byzantium, hardly more than a village, which Constantine later was to transform into his capital. In the next five years the emperor and his court made a series of sweeps from Nicomedia to Egypt and back.

The greatest of all sins is to upset things that have once been ordained and prescribed by our forefathers.
—DIOCLETIAN
Roman emperor

Constantine was a 13-year-old boy when he was sent to join the emperor Diocletian in A.D. 292. When Chlorus was reunited with his son 12 years later, he saw that Constantine had matured into a formidable soldier and leader.

A Roman medallion engraved with one of the more important scenes from the military career of Chlorus: his entrance into the city of London after the suppression of a revolt by the admiral of the Roman fleet.

The first eyewitness account of Constantine on record today was made by a Christian priest who saw the young officer in his uniform of bronze and scarlet standing by the emperor's side during one of their stops in Palestine. Writing down his impressions 40 years later, the priest remembered that Constantine, "already passing from childhood to adolescence, was matched by none in tallness, or in grace and beauty of form, and commanded the admiration of all who saw him."

While Diocletian, with Constantine in attendance, patrolled the Near East, his corulers were also moving their legions around — like the flexible mobile divisions of today. The coemperor Maximian crossed from Spain to North Africa to repel marauding Moors. Constantine's father, caesar of the west, sailed his Roman fleet in fog to Britain, defeated a usurper's army, and marched north to repair the former emperor Hadrian's defensive wall against invading Picts. Galerius, caesar of the east, was called to Armenia to rout the Persians, capturing, among other riches, the royal harem of the Persian king, who quickly sued for peace. Young Constantine took part in this campaign in order to gain experience in actual combat. Though only in his mid-teens, he had great physical strength (his soldiers admiringly called him Bullneck) and showed an early aptitude for command.

Relying on the excellent military performance of his three assistant rulers, Diocletian could concentrate on administration, his real interest, and address the economic difficulties he had inherited.

Hadrian's Wall, built on the orders of the Roman emperor Hadrian from A.D. 122 to 127, runs 73 miles across northern England. It was intended to protect England from the hostile Picts of Scotland. Chlorus oversaw extensive repairs to the wall during his time as caesar of the west.

Roman citizens line up to turn their money over to tax collectors. Diocletian refilled the empire's rapidly dwindling coffers by imposing crushing taxes on the populace.

Here his genius for governing gradually pulled things together. In the face of declining revenues and population, rising prices, hoarding by speculators, and trade at a standstill, Diocletian's iron rule kept the treasury full, the armies supplied, and the four imperial courts staffed and housed. Many people were pressed into repairing roads or transporting military goods without pay. Some fled from the tax collectors, whereas others stayed, only to be ground down into poverty. Overall, however, the empire's century of decline was halted by this remarkable emperor, and Constantine, his eventual successor, learned much from him.

Diocletian ruled for many years but became increasingly exhausted, irritable, and suspicious. Because his zeal to achieve a smoothly running empire did not allow for any disagreement, the dissidence of one group, the Christians, began to irritate him. Their refusal to worship the ancient gods of the empire led him to question their loyalty and patriotism. He began to blame them for anything that went wrong.

In the previous disaster-filled hundred years many Eastern religions, including Christianity, had swept through the empire. They offered personal mystical experiences that appealed to people's deepest emotions, strongly contrasting with the prosaic public ceremonies of Rome's ancient state religion. Many a Roman must have tapped his sandaled foot in boredom as he watched the state priests routinely offer sacrifices to ancient gods and long-gone deified emperors. These gods, whose statues adorned every public place in the empire, offered neither hope nor consolation to anxious individuals.

Roman society was ripe for a new faith, and Christianity, growing rapidly, provided it. Christians claimed that a humble preacher in the Roman province of Judaea was in reality the son of God; that he had risen from the dead after being crucified by the Roman governor Pontius Pilate; and that — miracle of miracles — he had returned briefly to earth and promised mankind that at the coming day of judgment he would reward believers with everlasting life. This message had more emotional appeal than other competing religions and was more immediate because Jesus had not been a remote deity but a real, living person. Busy Christian missionaries welcomed everyone into the new faith. Their message of God's love for all people and their many acts of charity toward widows, orphans, prisoners, and the poor made a deep impression. But their refusal to worship pagan gods put them in direct opposition to the emperor.

This behavior had not bothered more tolerant emperors of the first two centuries after Christ, although occasionally there had been sporadic anti-Christian outbursts and local pogroms in which Christian martyrs, refusing to recant, went bravely to horrible deaths. These martyrs had not been leading revolutions against the state; they paid their taxes, enjoyed the great benefits of Roman government, and suffered with everybody else in hard times. All they wanted was to keep church and state separate. No government could force them to make sacrifices to pagan gods they abhorred — or worse, to a deified emperor.

The image of a mother and child, perhaps representing Jesus and Mary, engraved in gold over sapphire blue glass. Such Christian artwork began to spread quickly throughout the Roman Empire in the second half of the 3rd century, signaling the growth of the radical new religion.

It was this rigid attitude that alarmed the conservative Diocletian, who was trying to revive Rome's power and rejuvenate its ancient religious traditions. He found it hard to believe that there were people not willing to go along with centuries-old ceremonies, largely expressions of patriotism, while carrying on their own private religious beliefs. The Christians' loyalty to Christ meant to him that they were not loyal to Rome.

Constantine, as an intimate member of the emperor's household, was a close observer of the emperor's growing antipathy. He must have been present at dinner-table arguments in which Diocletian's wife and daughter, who had become Christians in spite of Diocletian's opinions, expressed

A band of Christian martyrs-to-be have only prayer to defend them from the hungry lions of the Roman Colosseum. Diocletian, recognizing the ultimately subversive nature of Christianity, ushered in the Year of the Great Persecution in A.D. 303.

their point of view while Diocletian's colleague, the caesar Galerius, brutal son of a barbarian priestess, roared angrily that Christianity, if unopposed, would destroy the state.

Diocletian's patience finally gave out in A.D. 303, known as the Year of the Great Persecution. Incensed by his soothsayers' complaint that because the Christians had made the sign of the cross during a solemn public sacrifice the livers of the sacrificial animals could not be interpreted properly, he posted an edict ordering all Christians to sacrifice to the official pagan gods. When a high-spirited young Christian ripped down the edict, he was seized, tortured, and put to death. Three Christian palace officials, holding trusted positions on the

Roman soldiers prepare to offer a sacrificial bull to the pagan sun-god Mithras.

staff of Diocletian's own sacred bedchamber, were executed, as was the local bishop. Many other martyrs, particularly in the eastern half of the empire, fearlessly endured the most excruciating tortures as they died by burning, crucifixion, or strangling. Their heroism — some might call it fanaticism — was later immortalized when they were made saints by the Catholic church.

Constantine witnessed many of these examples of Christian courage. A brave young man himself, he was surely impressed by such bravery and may even

have wondered at the power of the Christian god
who could command such willing sacrifice. Any secret sympathy he felt might have been heightened
by news that his father, caesar of the west, had
shown restraint in obeying Diocletian's order, refusing to put to death any Christians in his area.
There is no evidence, however, that Constantine at
this time was drawn in any way toward Christianity
or that he did anything other than stand and watch
the terrible public persecutions. His position at Diocletian's court was far from secure and his life de-

pended entirely on the favor of the two eastern rulers. He knew that Galerius was jealous of his popularity with the soldiers and was waiting for him to make a wrong move. He knew also that Diocletian would not hesitate to have him killed for treason if he showed any Christian leanings. For the time being, and until his sudden conversion many years thereafter, he openly worshiped Mithras, the sun-god of the soldiers and also made sacrifices to the traditional Roman gods at all public ceremonies. Any temptation to switch religions must have been buried deep in his subconscious mind. But in his later years as a Christian emperor, he spoke of his predecessor's persecutions with horror.

Diocletian added other harsh measures, designed to break up Christian church services. He imprisoned clergy, destroyed Bibles, and demolished many of their places of worship — including a Christian building in Nicomedia that seemed to taunt him by its presence just outside the gates of the imperial palace. Within a short time that palace twice caught fire. Many years later Constantine asserted that the god of the Christians sent the lightning bolt that burned the palace to the ground. Diocletian, blaming Christian arsonists, increased his oppressive actions. In the far-off capital of Rome the quaking bishop Marcellinus (not all Christians were heroes) handed over his sacred books to the police. Prisons throughout the Near East, Egypt, and North Africa were filled to capacity with Christians innocent of any crimes.

Diocletian's frenzy was not to last. Within two years of his first edict against the Christians, he suffered from extreme exhaustion, caused by 20 years of constant stress. During the months of a very serious breakdown, with rumors flying about that he was dead, he had time to think seriously about retiring and leaving to others the burdens that had overwhelmed him. One of his problems was that the western coemperor Maximian had the strength but not the intelligence to take on these burdens. Diocletian solved this by sending him a secret order to abdicate on the same day that his own abdication would be made public.

> *How beautiful is the spectacle to God when a Christian does battle with pain, . . . threats, punishment, torture; when, mocking the noise of death, he treads underfoot the horror of the executioner; when he raises up his liberty against kings and princes and yields to God alone.*
>
> —MINUCIUS FELIX
> 3rd-century Latin writer
> and Christian apologist

In May A.D. 305 he arranged a formal abdication ceremony on a hill outside the walls of Nicomedia. Constantine, dressed in the scarlet-and-gold military uniform of a tribune, accompanied the court to hear the emperor's announcement. Standing beneath a tall column bearing the statue of his favorite god, Jupiter Optimus Maximus, Diocletian tearfully told the assembled legions that he had become infirm and needed rest. To their shouts of dismay he announced that he and his coemperor were abdicating and that Caesar Galerius would become the top-ranking augustus, ruling in the east. Chlorus, Constantine's father, would be the other augustus, ruling in the west. This was good news for his son, but he felt very far away from his father, the new coemperor, who was campaigning somewhere in the north of Europe.

Diocletian announced the names of two new caesars to take over the former roles of Galerius and Chlorus. Although only 25, Constantine may have hoped to hear his name, for his popularity with the troops and the flattering whispers of court in-

A Roman coin engraved with the image of Maximian Daia. Daia was appointed as one of the two new caesars upon the abdication of an exhausted Diocletian in May A.D. 305.

A northern view of the elaborate palace of the retired emperor Diocletian, located in what is now Split, Yugoslavia. The aged Diocletian spent the last years of his life wandering the massive corridors or dozing on the opulent terraces of his final home.

triguers during Diocletian's illness had led to rumors that he was in line for such a promotion. Instead, the new caesars turned out to be Severus and Daia, one an old army comrade of Galerius's, the other his nephew — neither particularly friendly to Constantine. A contemporary writer, Lactantius, described the reaction to this announcement:

> There was universal amazement. Galerius, thrusting back his hand, pushed Constantine aside and drew Daia forward, and having stripped him of the clothes he wore as a private citizen, stood him in the most conspicuous place. Everyone wondered who he could be. . . . Diocletian took off his purple robe, put it on Daia, and resumed his original name of Diocles.

Now a private citizen, the former emperor Diocletian retired to Salona (a colony on the island now known as Split) on the Dalmatian coast, where he supervised the building of an enormous and extravagant palace, still astonishing to tourists today. Here he tended his gardens and turned his back to the world.

Constantine could no longer count on Diocletian's protection. He was ambitious and confident of his ability, but in view of Galerius's jealousy and the fact that the new court was filled with Galerius's cronies, Constantine knew that his prospects for advancement were limited and that there might even be plots against his life. He began to plan his escape from the court.

4

Accession

Constantine, in Nicomedia, and his father, far away in Gaul, secretly corresponded about the new power structure. Both were aware of what the changed political lineup might mean to Constantine. More important, Chlorus's health was failing, and he was facing an important campaign in the north of Britain. He wrote to his coaugustus Galerius that he needed his son's help in his forthcoming campaign and requested his release.

The wily Galerius could not exactly refuse, but he could delay. Rumors had reached him about Chlorus's declining health. He was concerned about the possible death of Chlorus with his son at his side — followed, as in the old days, by his troops declaring Constantine emperor. The possibility of a vigorous young man suddenly and illegally in charge of such an enormous and important area did not appeal to him. He sent his coemperor Chlorus a series of excuses and continued to keep Constantine as a semihostage at his court. He knew that there was little that Chlorus could do about this because of the hundreds of miles of mountain ranges, rivers, and seas between Chlorus's headquarters in western Gaul and his son's quarters in Asia Minor.

> *Our aim has been . . . to see to it that the Christians . . . may come to their senses. . . . Such an obstinacy has possessed them, such a stupidity has overpowered them, that they will not follow those institutions which their own fathers called into being.*
> —GALERIUS
> Roman emperor

A medallion minted in Trier in A.D. 296 and engraved with the image of Chlorus as caesar. Chlorus was elevated to the position of augustus nine years later by Diocletian, and his new title opened up a world of fresh possibilities, and dangers, to his son, Constantine.

Galerius Valerius Maximianus, augustus of the east. Galerius was a cunning, violent man, and he represented a major threat to the political aspirations of the ambitious Constantine during the power struggle that followed the abdication of Diocletian.

Constantine realized that in order to reach his father he would have to devise a way of escaping from the well-guarded palace in Nicomedia, which was filled with soldiers, spies, and informers. He was so well known and his appearance so tall and striking that it would not be easy to leave without a permit from the emperor.

Everyone close to Galerius knew that he was in the habit of finishing all his official work in the late morning and then completely relaxing with a huge afternoon meal and many glasses of wine. At this time, the emperor would become pleasantly befuddled, and his usual suspicious and aggressive manner would temporarily disappear. Constantine picked such a moment to approach him with a request to join his father, and just as he had hoped, Galerius, in good humor, agreed, even putting the order in writing and allowing for the use of the government's relief horses along the imperial routes.

When Galerius finally awoke from his overindulgence late the following morning, he regretted what he had done, but it was too late. Constantine had not wasted any time. With a few trusted companions and swift horses, and with the emperor's order in his hands, he had left the palace promptly the day before, while still daylight, caught one of the many ferries that were rowed across the strait between Asia and Europe, and galloped through the night along the great Roman trunk route to points west. At the early posting stops the fugitives changed to the fresh horses so absentmindedly ordered by the emperor, then cut the hamstrings of any horses left behind. When the posse sent by the furious emperor arrived at the first staging post, it faced an infuriating delay. Fresh horses were hard to find, and by the next post the chase was given up entirely.

Constantine rode hard through the wild and rugged province of Dalmatia, where the smell of the air and the sounds of the forest brought back memories of his early childhood at his father's first army posts. His father now ruled supreme in this area, so that Constantine, impressive and commanding in the uniform of a military tribune, was no longer in danger. Perhaps he slowed his flight to stop off at the provincial town to which his mother, Helena, had retired after her divorce. She and her son would have embraced with emotion after their dozen years of separation, she, of course, having feared that she would never see him again. If Constantine did stop, his mother once more would have watched sadly as her only son disappeared from her life, this time to Gaul, where his father had a second wife, sons, and daughters—a bitter situation for her.

Constantine's hurried journey continued through lands completely new to him — the well-cultivated, fertile central lands of Gaul, with its calm, well-trafficked rivers, its people reflecting centuries of absorption of Latin culture. It was very different from the warmer, more luxurious, mainly Greek-speaking coastal provinces of the eastern empire.

He arrived at the channel port of Gesoriacum (modern Boulogne), from which his father intended shortly to sail with an army to Britain. The western emperor was greatly relieved at the safe arrival of his oldest son, whom he had last seen as a young teenager, now a fine-looking young man in magnificent health and vigor. But Constantine was shocked at his father's appearance. Always pale, Chlorus now had the look of a dangerously sick man.

They sailed with some reinforcements from Gaul across to a British port and then marched to York, the capital of Britannia, Rome's northernmost province. Even this city, with its rugged climate and its location at the edge of wild highlands and savage tribes, was a miniature Rome, with all the Roman comforts of hot baths, theaters, covered markets, and well-paved streets. Its walls were high and massive, with formidable towers for artillery projectiles and a splendid gateway through which well-trained troops would march to hurl back the wild Picts infiltrating across the border wall. From here Chlorus launched his last punishing expedition, his son fighting by his side. Then he came back to the city to die.

Chlorus spent his last days in his great imperial villa, from which, with his failing strength, he could see fields of flax and grain and, beyond, the barbarian wilderness. Father and son must have discussed many things of great importance. Constantine no doubt informed his father of Diocletian's recent persecutions and described the amazing fortitude of the Christian martyrs. His father in turn must have contrasted his own tolerance toward the many loyal Christians in his employ with Diocletian's ruthlessness. Although the two made their daily sacrifices to their ancestral gods and to the powerful soldier god of the Unconquered Sun, it is possible that Chlorus, facing death, wondered aloud about the Christian promise of forgiveness of sins, resurrection, and everlasting life. He told his son that he had even named one of his daughters — Constantine's half sister — Anastasia, or Resurrection, a Christian name. Certainly Chlorus must have had strong Christian sympathies that were impressed on the psyche of his sorrowing son.

Christian Europe may have begun with the march of Constantine's legions along the historic road from York to the port of London.
—LEONARD COTTRELL
English historian

54

In July of A.D. 306, Chlorus died in this far outpost of the western empire, having been in control there for only a year and a few months. The commander of his Frankish cavalry, which had been brought over to Britain (and whose tribal custom was to have the chief's son become the next chief), immediately proclaimed Constantine the new emperor. The regular Roman legions followed the familiar pattern of the previous century and shouted their agreement. Constantine was clothed in a purple robe and hailed as emperor. The news spread rapidly across the Channel to Europe. Whereas Gaul joined Britain in declaring for him, the other western provinces in Italy, Spain, and North Africa waited for the reaction of the legal emperor, Galerius.

The impregnable multiangular tower at York, Britannia, the northernmost outpost of the Roman Empire. Chlorus and Constantine used the fortress as a base from which to launch a series of punitive expeditions against the Picts.

A relief depicting an attack against a Roman outpost by a horde of barbarians. Such invasions were common on the outer reaches of the Roman Empire, and it was in these frontier battles that Constantine first proved himself as a warrior and leader.

Meanwhile, Constantine acted diplomatically. He and his dying father had probably foreseen — and perhaps even encouraged — the action of the troops. Chlorus's successful rule had been the result of patient and thorough planning, and his son was astute enough to follow his example. He was only 26, his prospects were excellent, and he had time to let others move rashly and make mistakes.

His first step was to seek Galerius's official approval of his accession, dispatching to the court at Nicomedia an announcement of his father's death

and a portrait of himself robed as augustus of the west and with an emperor's wreath of laurel around his brow. The furious Galerius knew that if he rejected Constantine's claim entirely there would be civil war. He therefore compromised, reducing Constantine's title to caesar and appointing Valerius Licinius, an older crony, as augustus to complete the tetrarchy (the rule of four).

Constantine accepted this demotion for the time being because he wished first to consolidate his power. Then he left Britain forever and set up headquarters in Trier, the frontier city where he had spent six happy years of his boyhood. In these familiar surroundings he began the campaign that was eventually to make him the first Christian emperor.

His first test was not long in coming. A Frankish tribe, which his father had permitted to settle in Gaul, suddenly revolted. By wintertime Constantine had crushed them, killing thousands and bringing back thousands of prisoners — including women and children — to fill Trier's huge amphitheater. A fifth- century historian praised this deed, reporting that the wild beasts in the arena had actually exhausted themselves in their attempts to slaughter so many barbarians.

With Gaul under control, Constantine made other moves to consolidate his power in the west. When Diocletian's former coemperor, the retired Maximian, proposed a marriage alliance with his daughter Fausta, Constantine agreed, knowing that the old man's name was still revered by many legions in Italy and Spain. Following his own father's pattern of putting his wife Helena aside for a more advantageous match, he first divorced a wife about whom nothing is known except her name — Minervina — and the fact that she was the mother of Constantine's son Crispus, a baby at the time of her dismissal. With this political maneuver behind him, he made a quick military foray into Spain, where the legions and the people acknowledged his rule promptly and with no resistance. Of the west, only Italy and the provinces of North Africa remained in the hands of others.

Constantine's popularity spread, and many people started to call him emperor, but as his power increased so did the resentment of his three colleagues. For six years a tricky game of power politics was played across the empire. Galerius, unlike the great Diocletian, did not have the skill to hold everyone's ambitions in check. Diocletian, now retired at his palace on the Adriatic Sea, must have been aghast as he watched his good work fall apart. Although many tried to persuade him to reenter the political world, he preferred to tend his cabbages

He . . . drove from his dominions, like wild and dangerous animals, those tribes he judged quite incapable of civilized living.
—EUSEBIUS
4th-century historian

and let others fight and maneuver for political power. By the year 310 there were four official emperors, including Constantine — because the title of caesar was abandoned as not carrying enough weight. Soon there were two more claimants to the four ruling positions, one being Constantine's meddling old father-in-law and the other his son, Maxentius, who seized most of Italy, including the great capital, Rome, and the food-producing province of North Africa.

In the early spring of A.D. 311, Constantine got the heartening news that his old enemy, the eastern emperor, Galerius, lay dying of a loathsome disease — eaten by worms, according to those Christians whom he was still persecuting viciously. On his deathbed Galerius, grabbing at any straw, issued an edict granting the Christians toleration if they would pray to their god for his health and the defense of the state. This change of heart came too late to save Galerius but also too late to rescind the edict. The death of Galerius meant that the great Christian persecution was over.

His death also led to a free-for-all among the existing claimants and others who entered the race for ultimate power. By the end of the year most of the aspirants had been removed by one means or another. In fact, Constantine "removed" his father-in-law, Maximian, when he was incautious enough to interfere with Constantine's ambitions, and planned to dispose of two other serious competitors as soon as possible. Getting rid of the first one, the recently appointed emperor of the east, Licinius, could be postponed until Constantine had the western half of the empire under his control. The other was more immediate — Maxentius, the son of Maximian. He controlled Italy and the capital city of Rome, guarded by special troops and tremendous walls. No one could claim to be supreme in the Roman Empire unless he had this ancient and revered city under his control.

Constantine's six years of careful jockeying had brought him to a critical point. A clever alliance with the eastern emperor, Licinius, left him free for a daring move, a march on Rome.

Maxentius, also claiming to be emperor, stood in the way of Constantine's ambition. He was killed when Constantine made his fateful march on Rome.

5

Under the Christian Banner

Constantine up to now had made his moves carefully. But in the year A.D. 312, driven by ambition to become the sole emperor of the west, he decided that it was time to lead an army over the Alps into Italy and defeat his rival Maxentius. Constantine's entire future, indeed his life, was at stake, for the loser in this showdown could expect no mercy.

The prospect for success was not encouraging. Unfamiliar with the land south of the Alps and the type of fighters likely to be encountered, Constantine's aides and generals advised him to abandon the plan. They feared that Maxentius's finely trained troops, a far cry from the usual barbarian enemies in the north, would be too great a match for Constantine's forces. Constantine's augurs, after studying chicken entrails to find out what the future would bring, were also pessimistic. But Constantine for once moved uncharacteristically. He knew that he would have to leave half his army behind to guard the Rhine border and that this would leave him about 40,000 men to march against three times as many in Italy. He knew that among Rome's defenders was the famed, well-trained Praetorian Guard.

> *With Christ's initials as a talisman, he went into battle against the blood-stained and dissolute tyrant, who sank in the deeps like a stone.*
> —EUSEBIUS
> 4th-century historian

A Roman coin engraved with the images of Constantine and the sun-god. Like most Romans of his day, Constantine had been taught to worship traditional pagan gods. But a spiritual dream on the night before the Battle of the Milvian Bridge changed the course of Constantine's life — and the course of history — forever.

A relief of the famed Praetorian Guard, the elite imperial bodyguards of Rome. As he approached Rome, Constantine had doubts about the ability of his own troops to defeat the guard, who were considered the finest fighters in the empire.

He had also heard of unusual cavalry units in northern Italy whose horses and riders were protected by a special armor copied from the Persians. But none of these things deterred him. Young, strong, and confident, he was eager to try out his skills on the battlefield.

Throughout the winter Constantine pressed his armorers to work overtime forging shields and weapons, including special iron-bound clubs to crush the opposing cavalry's new armor. His army, composed mostly of Britons, Gauls, and Germans who had settled in Gaul, trained daily. By early summer they were ready for the invasion of Italy.

Constantine led them through an Alpine pass, still patched with melting snow, into the blistering summer heat of the plains below. Large civilized cities lay in his way, guarded by detachments of Maxentius's army. Some put up stiff resistance, and Constantine's army suffered serious losses, but in the end the disciplined troops under his excellent generalship proved superior. The feared armored enemy cavalry had not learned proper tactics to match their new armor and were destroyed by Constantine's well-aimed maces. Most cities and towns fell to his lightning attacks. Those that held out changed their minds after receiving word of Constantine's mercy, for he had wisely forbidden his troops to sack and massacre. Soon the entire north of Italy came over to his side, and the way to Rome, the greatest city in the world, lay open.

Constantine then began to have secret misgivings. This is known because he later confessed to his biographer that as he approached Rome he felt unsure of himself. He also told this biographer a very different version of his famous vision — describ-

A coin bearing the Chi-Rho symbol, a monogram formed with the first two letters of the Greek word for Christ. Constantine and many of his officers painted the symbol on their shields and carried it into battle on the Milvian Bridge.

ing it as a cross in the sky seen by his entire army. This is the version that has appeared in countless textbooks and paintings, but most scholars have concluded that Constantine and his army saw no such thing before the gates of Rome. What he saw was what he told his son's tutor soon after his victory, while the vision and its direct effects were still vivid in his mind. He described to him a dream he had the night before the battle in which Jesus Christ appeared in his tent and directed him to put a monogram of Christ's name on the shields of his men. If he marched to battle under this talisman, he would be victorious.

Whether the dream was a miracle or an overwhelming psychological experience, Constantine believed that he had been in direct contact with the divine — in this case, the god of the Christians. He remembered that years before at Diocletian's court some Christians, by making the sign of the cross at a pagan religious ceremony, were believed to have ruined the prophecies of the court soothsayers. So now, in his nervous excitement before a crucial battle, he believed the guarantee of the Christian god

Instead of taking advantage of the fortified walls of Rome, Maxentius led his troops out of the city and marched to meet the oncoming forces of Constantine on the narrow Milvian Bridge.

that victory was certain if fought under his symbol. He did not have to seek a deeper meaning in Christianity at this time. He knew that Maxentius in his city stronghold was praying to Jupiter Maximus, the god of a thousand years of Roman victories. If the magic of the Christian god was greater than the magic of Jupiter, that was enough for him.

At dawn of the fateful October day of A.D. 312 a new note was added to the army's ordinary preparations for battle — a strange painted symbol not only on the elegant helmet of the commanding general but on the shields of many of his men. It was the first of many battles in history to be waged under the Christian banner.

As Constantine, with fanatical confidence, advanced toward Rome, he learned to his astonishment that Maxentius had left the shelter of Rome's great walls and had crossed the Tiber River, marching to meet Constantine along a narrow valley, with the river at his back. This was such bad generalship that Constantine needed no further proof that the powerful god of the Christians had caused Maxentius to lose his wits.

Maxentius's vanguard came into contact with
Constantine's advancing troops while the rest of his
army was still slowly crossing the two bridges that
spanned the Tiber — the narrow stone Milvian
Bridge and the still-narrower temporary bridge of
boats by its side. Constantine instantly realized that
he could outflank this slowly moving army. Taking
advantage of some low hills and the winding curves
of the river, he quickly hemmed the city's defenders
between them. His sudden attack broke the resistance of the front ranks and drove them back in
complete confusion, falling over their own support-
ing troops in their scramble to get back on the
bridges. The pontoon bridge broke under the weight
of hundreds of armored men, who struggled briefly
in the turbulent waters and then sank. In the wild
retreat, Maxentius was pushed off the Milvian

The forces of Constantine and those of Maxentius met head-on at the Milvian Bridge. Maxentius's force was quickly outflanked by Constantine's men, and in the panicked retreat that followed, Maxentius, his son, and many of his soldiers drowned in the Tiber.

Bridge and drowned. Soldiers later found his body floating in an eddy, cut off his head, and presented it to Constantine.

Maxentius was dead, his head mounted on a pike for the final march to Rome, but the death of this emperor is not what matters to history. Without Constantine's dream before the battle, his conquest would have been viewed as just one more pagan emperor defeating another, continuing that long, sad series of the previous century. As it was, the victory over his major enemy in the west convinced Constantine not only that his dream had proved the might of the Christian god but that Christianity was critical to his continued success. The inspiration that won him victory was to continue, strengthening his ambition to turn eastward and win other battles under the Christian banner.

6

The March on Rome

The gates of Rome, the greatest of pagan cities, opened before Constantine, the new Christian convert and now sole ruler of the western half of the Roman Empire. A delegation of uneasy senators welcomed the conqueror with obsequious and flattering speeches, adding official recognition to his conquest.

Crowds of people lined the parade route, observing with interest the grisly head of their former emperor brandished on a soldier's pike. They quickly forgot him as they cheered his tall, fine-looking successor and his curiously foreign-looking troops — men from far-off Britain, where, it was said, the sun never sets, and blond soldiers from the Rhine frontier whose fathers or grandfathers had been Rome's enemies.

Most of the spectators failed to understand the strange sign painted on Constantine's helmet, but Christians in the crowd recognized the monogram of Christ — the initials *CH* and *R* — written in the Greek alphabet common to the Christians of the east. Although Christians at the end of the third

The helmet of Constantine, the new ruler of the western Roman Empire, bears the talismanic Chi-Rho symbol. After the triumph of Constantine over Maxentius, the citizens of Rome were shocked to learn that the new emperor was a Christian.

century made up about a third of the city's population, most of them belonged to the lower or middle classes. They were of no importance politically and were looked down upon socially. What was a Christian sign doing on the helmet of a Roman emperor? Surely no one as splendid as he could ever be a Christian!

The marchers proceeded along the victory route — called the Sacred Way — of the age-old citadel, their feet following the steps of a thousand years of triumphant Roman generals and their troops. The avenue, paved with huge flagstones, led them past one breathtaking architectural display after another — theaters, basilicas, libraries, fountains, circuses, warehouses, public baths, law courts, and office buildings — all of unparalleled grandeur. The great stadium called the Colosseum — scene of gladiatorial combats and wild-beast shows — and the tall stone Column of Trajan, carved with more than a hundred spiraling scenes of military action, towered over the gawking troops. Most astonishing to these men from the frontier were the hundreds of apartment houses, some as high as seven or eight stories, that crowded around the private houses of the rich. They had occasional glimpses down dark and squalid side alleys but ignored them in favor of more inspiring sights along the world-famous route.

Gilded roofs of pagan temples gleamed from the heights of the city's seven hills, topped by the marchers' destination, the great temple of Jupiter Optimus Maximus, the supreme pagan god to whom all successful Roman generals always offered prayers of thanksgiving for victory. Constantine, a Christian for hardly more than a day, could not risk insulting the Roman people by refusing to comply with this ancient custom, but it must have been an ordeal for him. One can imagine his thoughts as he took part in the sacrificial pagan ceremony before Jupiter's awesome altar. Although pulled in one direction by Jupiter's traditional majesty, he was pulled more strongly in a new direction, convinced by his easy victory that a more powerful god had given him a mission to dethrone Jupiter forever. For the moment, however, he was careful to hide his turmoil of spirit.

As they marched into Rome, Constantine's troops encountered the Column of Trajan, a 97-foot marble shaft covered with minutely detailed narrative reliefs depicting the Roman emperor Trajan's victories over barbarian armies.

The Senate, eager to show him honor, awarded him the title of supreme augustus, thereby insulting the other two equally ambitious emperors in the east. The Senate also ordered the late emperor Maximian's statues and inscriptions to be destroyed and his laws removed from the record books. They then voted their new emperor a statue seven times life size and a triumphal arch to be placed near the Colosseum. The Arch of Constantine, which tourists can see today, was erected hurriedly. Pieces of borrowed sculpture were inserted here and there, and the rest was carved in a stiff and rigid style by sculptors who lacked the skills of the artists of earlier centuries. The inscription on the arch was ambiguous, referring to Constantine's victory "through divine inspiration," a phrase that avoided the unthinkable — that their emperor's divine vision had not been pagan but Christian.

For a while Constantine had to postpone much contact with the Christian community in Rome while he tackled urgent administrative problems. The previous century of inflation, wars, and taxes had drained Rome of jobs and vitality. Once a city of about 1,500,000 inhabitants, Rome's population had shrunk to half that amount. Many families were unemployed and on relief, supported by the city's

The citizens and public officials of Rome gathered at the Forum to await the arrival of Constantine. The populace was eager to welcome the new hero and were not offended by the sight of the previous emperor's severed head being carried along on a pike.

huge dole of free flour and other staples. Skilled workmen and highly trained civil servants had left the city in search of better jobs in other cities of the empire, such as Trier and Nicomedia, both preferred by recent emperors.

Constantine realized that the city of Rome had become a backwater, even though it was still the official capital of the empire and the site of its most ancient legislative body, the Senate. And the more he saw of the snobbish, aristocratic senators, the more he despised them as essentially useless, fulfilling their mostly ceremonial role with insufferable self-satisfaction and pride. They in turn secretly looked down on him as a man of little culture or refinement. They considered his sudden interest in Christianity an outrage to their ancestral customs and hoped that it would be a passing phase.

In this they were to be stunningly surprised. According to the Italian historian Andrew Alfoldi, "Revolutionary plans were already fermenting in his brain." Constantine knew that he could not afford to offend the people of Rome by ordering them to give up their ancient pagan religion overnight in favor of Christianity. He would have to move slowly and carefully in order to make Christianity the religion of the Roman world.

73

Constantine realized that he actually knew little about Christian thought and practice. Before he could effect the drastic changes he had in mind, he would have to seek out Rome's bishop and others of the Christian community for guidance in matters as basic as learning Christian prayers and attending Christian services. The Christians of the Roman community were startled by the sudden, unexpected interest of their new emperor and could hardly believe their luck.

There had been Christians in Rome for almost 300 years. In the early days of Emperor Nero (A.D. 37–68) when they were a very small group, they had been blamed for a great fire that destroyed much of the city. In the persecutions that followed, two vis-

The Arch of Constantine was built in honor of the new emperor immediately following his entrance into Rome. The monument was constructed in a hurried and haphazard manner, however, and does not compare with earlier Roman sculptures.

iting Christian preachers, Peter and Paul — later to become two of the church's greatest saints — were martyred and buried in Christian cemeteries outside of Rome's walls, where their simple tombs soon became shrines. Since that time, Christians, although growing in numbers, had tried to worship inconspicuously, so much so that pilgrims visiting the city would not have been able to find a Christian church among the city's temples. Christian meetings took place either in houses and apartments in the city or on small pieces of land in the countryside beyond the city walls. Because Roman law forbade the burial of anyone, from emperor to slave, within the ancient city walls, Christian burials took place in the suburbs. One of their earliest burial grounds,

The gold bottom of an early Christian glass bowl is engraved with the images of the apostles Peter and Paul. The two followers of Jesus were put to death by the Roman emperor Nero in A.D. 37.

south of Rome on the Appian Way, was at a place called Catacumbas, where they constructed underground tombs and tomb chambers in layers to make the most economical use of expensive real estate. These are the catacombs of today.

When Constantine was shown the various places used for Christian services and worship, he was appalled by their simplicity. Even the most sacred sites, the tombs of St. Peter and St. Paul, were hardly more than small sheds holding pilgrims' offerings. Constantine was used to imperial show, to ornate palaces and lavish ceremonies. He had no intention of worshiping in such embarrassingly modest places and immediately resolved to construct churches worthy of his attendance. By so doing, he intended to alter the public image of Christianity.

Constantine challenged his architects to design the kind of church that would not only fit the needs of Christian worship but would show the world the splendor of the Christian god. He insisted on a grand scale, the scale of emperors. An excellent model, the basilica, lay at hand — a long, windowed, multipurpose hall, roofed with timber or tiles, that had evolved through the centuries for various public uses, such as drill hall, law court, or throne room for imperial audiences. The architects concluded that with a few alterations they could easily adapt the basilica's basic framework for the seating of Christian congregations and the various Christian rituals. As they started to work on various plans, Constantine looked around for appropriate sites.

Constantine might have wanted to build grand churches in the very center of the ancient city, designed to outshine all its pagan temples, but doing so would have antagonized the Senate and most of the population. A huge Christian church suddenly placed by the Forum or the Temple of Jupiter would create riots and risk destruction of the new church — and Constantine's career, as well. So he turned instead to imperial estates on the edge of the city and found among them excellent sites on which Christian structures could dominate the landscape for many miles.

On one of these estates was an imperial palace, which he turned over to the astonished bishop of Rome, Militiades — a historical precedent. Though the bishop at this time was no more important than bishops of other large Roman cities, his successors were later to become popes, accustomed to the princely style that Constantine had demanded. But at the time it must have been difficult for Militiades, accustomed to a simple house, to adjust suddenly to a huge palace.

An ornate crypt at Catacumbas, the location of an early Christian burial ground outside Rome. Until Constantine came to power, Christian burial was a very modest affair, but as Christianity gained importance the burial ritual became much more elaborate.

One of Constantine's first projects in Rome was the creation of this magnificent basilica, the first St. Peter's Cathedral, named in honor of the martyred apostle Peter. This building was the center of Christian pilgrimages for a thousand years.

Next to the bishop's new residence were the barracks of the horse guards, which Constantine ordered razed. In their place, among villas and gardens, Constantine ordered construction to begin on the first Christian cathedral, the Church of St. John Lateran, intended to outshine any pagan temple in Rome. In the double aisles of this monumental building were columns of rare red, green, and yellow marble. The vault in the enormous apse at one end was overlaid in gold and lit by oil lamps of gold and silver. A silver canopy hung above a statue of Christ on his throne, surrounded by statues of his angels and apostles. A solid silver table served as the church's first altar, and the baptistry had a solid silver font.

ALVMNVSVIC IDEVSR CALLIMORIVS
VSEVIC
MAZICINVS SER PENIIVS

At the same time, Constantine ordered a second church to be built over the modest tomb of the martyred St. Peter, nearby on Vatican hill. This church, which became the most famous church in Christendom, was built in the same splendid style, with the saint's shrine set off by four twisted marble columns and an ornate canopy bathed in light filtering down from high windows.

These two churches achieved Constantine's goal of magnificence and ostentation and something more: Their floor plan and exteriors, following the design of a classical basilica, inadvertently set the style of Christian churches for centuries to come.

Constantine did not remain to oversee their construction. Perhaps when he had first entered Rome as conqueror, he had intended to live there and make it the official residence of the emperor of the west, but its evident stagnation and the stiff-necked attitudes of its pagan upper classes made him change his mind. In January A.D. 313, after treating the public to gladiatorial games and wild-beast shows, Constantine left the city without regret. But he had succeeded, more than he knew, in making an indelible Christian imprint upon Rome's ancient pagan face.

Gladiators fend off wild animals and fight one another in Rome's Colosseum. Despite the improvements effected by his architects, engineers, and artisans, Constantine found Rome a dreary place, and after appeasing the public with gory spectacles like the ones pictured here, he gratefully took his leave.

7

The Most Powerful Man on Earth

Constantine and his court, which now included Christian teachers and priests, headed back to Trier, a city he infinitely preferred to Rome. On his way north he had a meeting with Licinius, the successor to Galerius as augustus of the east. Licinius had heard of Constantine's ruthless removal of the emperor Maxentius and wanted to make sure that Constantine had no such plans for him.

Constantine reassured Licinius of his peaceful intentions. Although he secretly believed that his new god planned more conquests for him, he needed time to oversee his new western territories before he waged another war. The two men worked out a treaty agreeing to respect each other's vast borders. Constantine also persuaded Licinius to agree to a joint edict granting "Christians and everyone else the right freely to follow whatever rule of faith they choose." This general pronouncement of religious toleration, called the Edict of Milan, was Constantine's first step toward his ultimate goal of creating a Christian empire.

He certainly felt himself to be the bishop of all mankind, a God-appointed Pope.
—ANDREW ALFOLDI
Italian historian

A gravestone relief found in Trier depicts a domestic scene from everyday life in the city. Constantine considered Trier to be his true home, and after conquering Rome he hastened there and joined his growing family.

81

Constantine's favorite sister, Constantia, might have worn her hair after the fashion of this 4th-century aristocratic woman.

To cement their alliance, a marriage was arranged between Licinius and Constantine's favorite half-sister, Constantia. Everyone was relieved that these two powerful emperors, now brothers-in-law, had made peace. But in reality a clash was inevitable.

Soon after their meeting, Licinius heard that his subordinate caesar of the east, the one called Daia, had crossed over the straits of the Bosporus into Europe with an army and had occupied the fortified village of Byzantium at the entrance of the Black Sea. This was in Licinius's territory. Licinius, a good general, moved his troops swiftly eastward and routed and killed his disloyal colleague, returning in triumph to his imperial eastern capital, Nicomedia. Now, instead of the four emperors of the previous year, there were only two — Licinius and Constantine—ruling the Roman world.

Meanwhile, Constantine returned to his huge imperial palace in Trier. Waiting to welcome him were his wife, Fausta, her growing family of sons and daughters, and Crispus, his oldest son by his first wife. Constantine added a Christian tutor to this big household. From that moment, all of Constantine's children were brought up as Christians.

Constantine's religious fervor grew stronger every day. He invited many Christian dignitaries, including a bishop from Spain, to join his staff. As an uneducated, barely literate man, Constantine was impressed with their learned theological discussions even though he understood little of them. As a good administrator, he was pleased to discover the excellent organization of the Christian church in every city throughout the Roman world and realized that under his protection and encouragement it could become a powerful political force. To the delight of his new Christian advisers, Constantine exempted the clergy from military service, taxes, and compulsory labor for the state. He granted bish-

Constantine had his architects build many grand structures in Trier, including an imperial palace and this massive basilica. Soon, however, the Christian emperor set his sights on a city in the east — Byzantium.

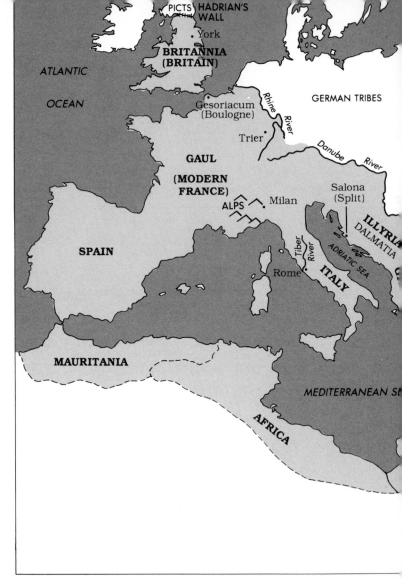

ops the right to judge cases within the church. He
sent funds from his imperial treasury to Christian
parishes all over the empire and built them splendid
churches—an annoyance to his pagan coemperor.

As Licinius saw the new confidence and increas-
ing wealth of the Christians, his old fears of Christian subversion were revived, and he demanded that
Christians make public pagan sacrifices as a show
of loyalty to him.

For ten years (A.D. 314–324) an uneasy truce ex-
isted between the two emperors. Both used the
breathing space to strengthen their borders and

GOTHS

Naissus (Niš)

BLACK SEA

Serdica (Sofia)

THRACE

Constantinople

Nicomedia

Nicaea

ASIA MINOR

ARMENIA

PERSIAN EMPIRE

MESOPOTAMIA

SYRIA

Euphrates River

PALESTINE

JUDAEA

Jerusalem

PERSIAN GULF

EGYPT

Alexandria

Nile River

RED SEA

ARABIA

By A.D. 323 the Roman Empire was under the control of two rulers: Constantine in the west and Licinius in the east. It was only a matter of time before the two emperors clashed.

build up their armies. Constantine, however, moved the seat of his administration eastward to Serdica (modern Sofia in Bulgaria), close to a part of Licinius's territory in northern Greece. He also threatened Licinius by enlarging a nearby naval base. Now all that he needed was a reason, other than his own ambition, to invade the east and add it to his rule. Licinius's mistreatment of the Christians did not give Constantine sufficient political excuse to cross the border between them, but when barbarian tribes invaded Licinius's territory, he chose to look upon their action as a threat to his adjacent lands

A coin engraved with the likeness of the ruler of the eastern Roman empire, Licinius. Although he was Constantine's brother-in-law, Licinius was wary of his powerful neighbor to the west, and rightly so: In A.D. 323 Constantine invaded his territory.

in the west. Near enough to react quickly, Constantine led his troops across his coemperor's borders, easily repelling the invasion. Many people, particularly the Christians, sang his praises and proclaimed him the sole defender of the empire.

Licinius could not allow this violation of his boundary and in A.D. 324 declared war. With justification he called his war a defensive war, but Constantine chose not to see it that way. He sincerely believed that he was not an aggressor but a crusader on a mission to save the Christians in the east. He had even come to believe that God had chosen him as his representative as far back as 18 years before, in Britain, when his father's soldiers had acclaimed him emperor. Now his Christian advisers reinforced this belief, calling him the new Moses, God's champion, while calling Licinius a madman possessed by devils.

Constantine wrote: "God decreed my service. Setting out from the sea in Britain and the lands where the sun sets, I have driven out the terrors that ruled on every land. Convinced of my glorious task, I come also to the lands of the East, which in their bitter pains, require my aid."

Licinius brought the bulk of his army from Asia over the straits into his province of Thrace, where he waited for Constantine's next move. He also ordered his best naval vessels, a fleet of 350 swift *triremes* (warships rowed by three banks of oars), to prevent any of Constantine's troop and supply ships from sailing through the Hellespont, the narrow waterway between Europe and the Asian shores.

Constantine massed his army on the Thracian border and prepared to attack. The coming civil war was to engage almost 300,000 men, more than in any battle for another 1,000 years. It also involved important naval action. Constantine had withdrawn his son Crispus from the Danube frontier and put him in charge of a fleet of military transports and supplies. These were to force their way through the enemy's naval defense of the strait, resupply Constantine's land forces, and blockade the enemy's escape route to Asia.

A fleet of Roman warships, under the command of Constantine's son, Crispus, broke through Licinius's naval blockade of the Hellespont and delivered crucial supplies to Constantine's army.

Before the battle, Constantine, in full view of his troops, entered his portable chapel-tent to pray to the Christian god for another great victory. According to his biographer Eusebius, he soon received an encouraging divine command. Inspired, he moved quickly to lead his waiting army. His special battle standard, topped with a gold cross carrying the initials of Christ, was held high in the midst of his bodyguard of 50 men. All believed that this standard was so powerful that no one near it could be harmed. The sight of the tall, magnificently armored emperor under the protection of his famous talisman made his entire army confident of victory.

The eastern emperor Licinius prayed at a pagan shrine and then exhorted his men to defeat those who had betrayed the religion of their ancestors. Both commanders recognized the importance of the impending showdown between the pagan gods and the Christian god.

The two armies clashed on a broad plain. Though Licinius and his troops fought bravely, Constantine was the better general, with better soldiers, experienced veterans of tough frontier wars against Germans and Goths. After the battle, these veterans told tales of the magical power of their emperor's Christian battle standard — how it intercepted missiles and disheartened the enemy at whatever section of the battlefield it appeared. By the end of the day Licinius and his forces had fallen back to the seaport of Byzantium, where they prepared for a long siege. This old walled village, on a narrow point of land, was protected on three sides by water. Supplies from Asia could easily be rowed to it across the narrow channel of the Bosporus.

During the siege, as Constantine waited for his son's warships to cut off Licinius's escape route to the east, he had time to admire the excellent defensive situation of Byzantium. It is probable that at this time he decided that once he had defeated Licinius and become the sole emperor he would enlarge and strengthen its fortifications so that no future enemy could occupy its strategic site and cut the empire in half. Only a few months later, when considering the best place for his new imperial capital, he realized that a rebuilt Byzantium would serve his interests.

When the sails of Crispus's war fleet appeared on the horizon, Licinius knew the game was up. He was able to escape across the straits and make a last stand when Constantine pursued him. After his second defeat in battle, on September 18, A.D. 324, he fled to his old capital of Nicomedia, but his days were numbered. Although he sent his wife, Constantia, to beg her half brother to spare his life, her tears were not sufficient, and he was executed. Constantine could not risk a living challenger to his God-appointed power, nor did his version of Christianity include compassion or forgiveness.

For the first time in nearly 40 years, since Diocletian in A.D. 286 gave up the attempt to rule alone, the empire was united under a single emperor, Flavius Valerius Constantinus — the name soon inscribed on all the coins of the realm.

At last Christians not only could live without fear throughout the empire, but their religion would be shared and encouraged by the most powerful man on earth. Soon after his final victory, Constantine ordered restitution to all Christians who had been persecuted. Prisoners condemned to gang labor in the mines or to digging ditches were set free and given their former jobs. Exiles returned, and their homes were restored to them. Churches that had been vandalized or destroyed were rebuilt, often far more splendidly than before.

At the same time that he was attending to the Christians in his realm, Constantine also began to rebuild the old seaport of Byzantium for use as his capital. His predecessors had chosen favorite cities and rebuilt them extravagantly to suit their personal imperial image. Constantine intended his capital, at the crossroads of two continents, to be the biggest and best of them all. The grand old ancient capital, Rome, with its centuries of glorious buildings crowding its famous seven hills, was still vivid in his memory. His new city would be as grand as Rome, with its many impressive public struc-

> *God has committed to my guardianship the administration of all earthly affairs by his heavenly will.*
> —CONSTANTINE

tures — but there would be important differences. It would be a Christian city from the start, with churches instead of pagan temples gleaming from its hills. It would be a vital city, in the center of things, unlike old Rome, now stagnating on the sidelines. And it of course would be named after him —Constantinople, the city of Constantine.

English historian Edward Gibbon describes how Constantine himself marked out its boundaries:

On foot, with a lance in his hand, the Emperor himself led the solemn procession, and directed the line which was traced as the boundary of the destined capital, till the growing circumference was observed with astonishment by the assistants, who at length, ven-

Romulus, the mythical founder of the city of Rome, traces its sacred borders with a pair of oxen. Constantine used this traditional method to expand the seaport town of Byzantium into his new holy city — Constantinople.

tured to observe that he had already exceeded the most ample measure of a great city. "I shall advance," replied Constantine, "till He, the invisible guide who marches before me, thinks proper to stop."

Work on the city of Constantinople started in A.D. 324 and continued for six years. High sea walls and land walls stretched more than two miles west of the old fortified port. Architects from all over the empire began to design huge public structures, avenues, and gardens. A magnificent palace and audience hall, grander than any in memory, began to take shape. From its awesome imperial throne Constantine intended to rule the Roman world not only as emperor but as leader of the Christian church.

8
Christianity and the Empire

While Constantine's new capital was rising on the shores of the Bosporus, a serious controversy erupted within the Christian church. During their three centuries of existence, Christians had spread out to all corners of the empire and even beyond it. They had operated, often surreptitiously, in small, isolated groups and had studied different versions of the Bible, had different oral traditions, and distinctive local ways of conducting services and interpreting the Christian message. Now that Christianity had become an authorized — in fact, a state-subsidized — religion, its bishops recognized the need for a common creed. As they sought to write one that all could approve, violent disputes erupted in many Christian communities. The worst took place in Egypt, where an Alexandrian priest named Arius argued that Jesus Christ was distinct and not the same as God. This was heresy to those who held the orthodox view that Christ and God were one and the same.

> *Constantine's character and methods had so profound an influence on his world that some historians claim that with his accession, ancient history ended and the Middle Ages began.*
> —J. H. SMITH
> Constantine biographer

A drawing of Constantine from a 15th-century Ethiopian manuscript emphasizes his sword and his militancy under the mantle of Christianity.

On May 25, A.D. 325, at the bidding of Constantine, bishops from all over the empire gathered at the town of Nicaea to hammer out a universally accepted creed for the rapidly expanding Christian religion.

Constantine, convinced that he had been chosen by God to rule not only the world but all the Christians in it, decided to put an end to this show of disunity. He invited the bishops of the empire, at public expense, to a conference in Nicaea, a city in Asia Minor (modern Turkey).

The famous Council of Nicaea, the first worldwide conference of Christian churches, was solemnly convened on May 25, A.D. 325. About 250 bishops assembled in a splendid audience hall. Most had come from the Greek-speaking provinces of the east, but a few had traveled long distances from points

west, and one had even come from Persia — a rival empire. These unworldly men had been living modestly, expecting few treasures on earth and looking for rewards only in heaven. Now they had been honored by a warm invitation from the emperor of the Roman world.

When Constantine appeared, an enormous man in glittering tiara and purple robes, the bishops rose to their feet in awe and respect. He told them to be seated, that he, too, was a bishop, appointed by the Lord, and had come among them to learn and listen. Moved by the lame legs and burned hands of those who had survived persecution, he walked slowly around the chamber to greet each one, even kissing the empty eye sockets of a blinded bishop.

Constantine's humble attitude, quite out of character, did not last long. After listening for two months to heated, long-winded arguments that he did not understand about the nature of God, he made it clear that he would no longer tolerate stubborn insistence on what he considered small and unimportant points. He demanded unity, expressed in a single acceptable creed. The fearful bishops, unwilling to risk their protector's wrath, produced and signed the Nicene Creed, which, with some variations, is familiar to Christians today:

> We believe in one God, the Father Almighty, the Maker of all things visible and invisible. And in one Lord Jesus Christ, only-begotten Son of the Father by Whom also all things were made, Who for our salvation was made flesh and lived among men, and suffered, and rose again the third day, and ascended to the Father, and will come again in glory to judge the living and the dead. And we believe also in one Holy Spirit.

Fausta, the emperor's wife, was murdered by her husband in A.D. 326. Her end was particularly cruel; Constantine had the heat in her steam bath turned up until she was scalded to death.

Along with his wife, Constantine had his first son, Crispus, put to death. The motive for these acts has been lost to history, but the acts themselves reveal a darker side of the Christian emperor.

By the end of summer the bishops had made an important start on drawing up rules for the management of a universal Catholic church. These included discipline of the clergy, election of bishops, the date of Easter — matters that had been decided locally until this first convocation. When the group disbanded, Constantine gave them a state banquet in which they reclined on couches and were served by slaves. Dazzled by their treatment, they returned to their posts with renewed vigor.

The following year, A.D. 326, marked the passing of 20 years since Constantine had been acclaimed emperor by his troops in Britain. He decided to follow the custom of previous emperors by celebrating his anniversary in Rome, the city still considered the capital of the world by all the people of his empire. Although he had become a Christian, he still retained the important title of pontifex maximus, chief priest of the empire's pagan gods. He hoped that by observing Rome's traditional rites of thanksgiving he could lessen the hostility of Rome's pagan aristocrats.

A late-13th-century mosaic of Constantine and his mother, Helena. Helena reappeared at her son's side shortly after he murdered his wife and eldest son. Constantine gave her the title of empress dowager.

But this was not to happen. In the year 326 he ordered two inexplicable and tragic murders, followed by an equally inexplicable public tantrum in Rome. Contemporary Christian writers, shocked by the sudden cruelty and instability of their leader, made little if any mention of these murders, so only the barest facts have survived. All that is known is that before Constantine reached Rome he had ordered the murder of his brilliant oldest son Crispus, and soon after, the murder of his second wife, Fausta — by turning up the heat in her steam bath. There was gossip of Crispus's treason or of his adultery with Fausta, but gossip — instead of facts — is all that remains. All statues of them were promptly destroyed, all inscriptions chiseled away so that history would forget them.

By the time Constantine reached Rome, with these two horrifying murders on his mind, he was in such a state of remorse, guilt, or anger that he ruined the elaborate ceremonies the city had planned for him. When leading the procession of

thanksgiving to the Temple of Jupiter, he suddenly broke into a fit of fury and refused to proceed. He cut short his stay in the ancient city, vowing never to return. From then on he was determined that his new city, Constantinople, would take the place of backward-looking Rome.

When Constantine returned to the east, his mother, Helena, came with him. After many years of quiet retirement she had reemerged into public life, with the imposing title of empress dowager. She had become an enthusiastic Christian, proud of her son's achievements for the church and eager to do her part in advancing its growth. In 327, possibly to atone for the two murders and the fiasco in Rome, she proposed to visit the Holy Land as her son's ambassador. Constantine enthusiastically agreed, writing the bishop of Jerusalem to look after her and show her his most sacred sites. He also told the bishop that he would pay for the construction of great churches on these sites to take the place of humble shrines.

Constantine loves to show himself as sweet and charming, but on occasion all of a sudden he strikes and savages.
—PHILOSTORGIUS
4th-century historian

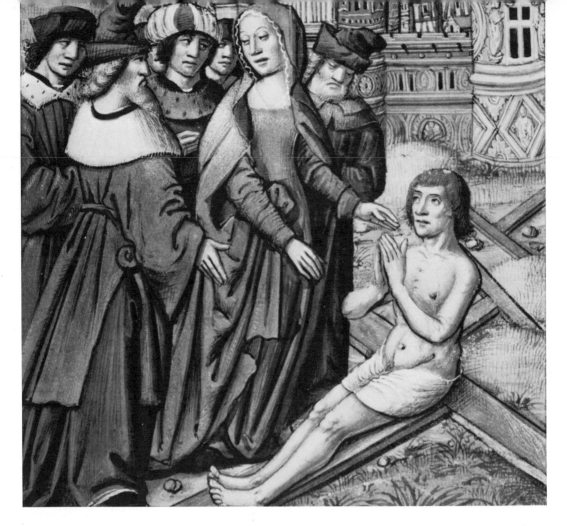

While Constantine's mother was in Jerusalem, she discovered the remnant of what she claimed was the "true cross" of Jesus Christ. This medieval manuscript embellishes the story, suggesting that she also found the risen Christ.

Helena (later St. Helena) thus became the first official pilgrim to the Holy Land. Most historians have assumed that she was in her sixties, considered old in those days, and she seems to have been very energetic for her age. She was determined to find the site of Christ's tomb and was convinced that she had done so after unearthing a cave where, tradition said, Christ's body had been placed. Her workmen also dug at the place where Christ had been crucified and found huge pieces of wood, with nails attached, which she identified as the cross. Delighted by this miracle, she sent pieces of the wood to many churches and to her son, Constantine, who enshrined them as relics. He also made some of the nails into a bridle for his war-horse to ensure more Christian victories in battle.

Helena supervised the beginnings of a beautiful basilica, the Church of the Holy Sepulcher, using the rarest marbles for its columns and gold foil for its ceilings. In addition, she ordered the construction of other churches at important early Christian sites such as Bethlehem. These churches in the Holy Land, unchanged for centuries, became the important destinations for Christian pilgrims from many lands. Her mission accomplished, Helena returned to her son. Years after her death in about 330, she was made a saint by the Catholic church.

Constantine was determined to make his adopted capital the rival of Rome, and by A.D. 330 the town of Byzantium had been transformed into a glorious monument to Christianity — Constantinople. It was said that the city was beautiful enough to be presented to the Virgin Mary herself, as Constantine does in this mosaic.

During the years that Helena was transforming sites in the Holy Land, Constantine's architects were also transforming the sleepy town of Byzantium into a magnificent capital. Although Constantine was through with Rome, its fame was still so great that he tried to make his new Rome a copy of the old. Within an area jutting like a thumb into the sea and encircled by miles of high walls, he built a forum, a chariot-race course, law courts, amphitheaters, baths, workers' apartments, and mansions for the rich. Much as he had despised Rome's do-nothing, snobbish senators, he built a new Senate building and created equally powerless senators to fill it. His agents scoured the empire's temples for gold and silver treasures, even ripping off bronze temple doors and roofs to adorn the new buildings. Famous statues from Greece, Egypt, and Syria suddenly appeared in prominent places on Constantinople's wide avenues.

But in one important respect the new city differed from old Rome. It was to be a Christian city, free from any taint of paganism. Instead of pagan temples there rose abbeys, priories, and church schools. Most splendid of all were two cathedrals dedicated to the apostles and to peace.

On May 17, A.D. 330, Constantine dedicated his new capital. Looking like an Oriental potentate in jewel-encrusted purple robes and a pearl-studded diadem on his elegantly curled long hair, he accepted the homage of the crowds parading before his imperial box. From that moment, Constantinople grew in glory, and old Rome's decline and decay accelerated.

Constantine had seven more years to live. His greatest achievements were behind him, but he used his remaining years to consolidate the gains he had made as single ruler of the Roman world. No other Roman emperor except Augustus Caesar ruled longer or with greater effect on history.

An excellent administrator, Constantine brought economic order to his empire. His taxes were harsh but effective, paying for his vast building programs, the defense of his frontiers, and the maintaining of lifelines vital to trade. He even achieved a sound

currency through the introduction of a gold coin (the solidus) of unchanging purity and weight.

Constantine was also a superb commander in chief. He inspired loyalty in his fighting men, so much so that in 30 years of his reign he was never threatened by rebellion in the ranks. When barbarian tribes in the Balkan region increased their raids, he built strong battlements along the frontiers and sent well-trained armies to contain and harass them. Such protection enabled the empire to thrive, particularly in the east, where the new great trading center, Constantinople, brought great wealth and prestige.

As Constantine grew older, his knife-edged temper and irascibility increased, along with his sense of self-importance. He gained 50 pounds, which he concealed under stiff, ornate robes instead of the softer imperial togas of previous centuries. Isolated from the common run of men by his own sense of omnipotence, he insisted that petitioners had to

The emperor kneels as he is baptized in the final year of his life, A.D. 337. Constantine hoped that the holy waters of baptism would wash his most grievous sins — the murder of his wife and son — from his soul.

Evidence supports the claim that as Constantine grew older he gained as much as 50 pounds. This coin from the last years of his reign depicts Constantine as an older and somewhat heavier man.

prostrate themselves before him and kiss the hem of his skirts. His enormous palace, containing hundreds of rooms and halls, was run by a chief chamberlain and his staff, usually eunuchs recruited from Armenia or Persia, where castration was legal. These suave, Greek-speaking servants contrasted oddly with the rough, heavily armed German guards posted throughout the dark corridors of the palace to protect the person of his sacred majesty.

In his last years the power of the church grew steadily. Constantine not only underwrote its finances but was a master of publicity on its behalf. Inscriptions in every town proclaimed that Christ had chosen the emperor Constantine to rule the world under his name. Constantine's portrait on coins and statues and paintings showed the gaze of "the most religious majesty" directed heavenward.

Late in life he tried his skill in preaching sermons and defining the nature of God, but his intellect did not match his other gifts. His exhortations on behalf of Christianity and his letters to members of the clergy were filled with long words tumbling all over each other in disordered fashion. He was the despair of his secretaries, taking much too much time to get to whatever point he was trying — often unsuccessfully—to make.

He also undertook to express Christian ideals in some of his laws. Poor parents were to be given food and clothing for their unwanted children so that they would not sell them into slavery or leave them on dunghills to die. He banned crucifixion and branding of the face, "because man is made in God's image."

To obey God's command to rest on the seventh day he chose "the venerable day of the Sun" — our Sunday — which also had a useful meaning to those pagans who had worshiped the sun-god and could thus transfer their prayers more easily.

In A.D. 337, Constantine felt that death was approaching, and he asked to be baptized — a necessary step if all his sins were to be forgiven. Although he believed that he was the chosen servant of God and as such ought to be welcome in heaven, he nevertheless may have had a nagging, guilty feeling that his venomous family murders were mortal sins — not forgivable except through baptism. The bishop of Nicomedia, officiating at his baptism, watched the awesome emperor exchange his jeweled finery for the simple white dress of a Christian novice.

Constantine died on May 22, A.D. 337, confident that God would now accept him in heaven as his 13th apostle. His embalmed body lay on a solid gold catafalque in the great hall of his palace in Constantinople. Throughout the summer, crowds of mourners filed by. The government, while waiting for Constantine's three sons to arrive, continued certain rituals — presenting petitions to the corpse as if it were still alive. The court chamberlain greeted the late emperor each morning and said good night to him each evening. Then Constantine's body was placed in a tomb designed to show him as the 13th apostle, with the carved figures of Christ's other apostles kneeling in reverence, six on a side.

The pagans throughout the empire mourned him as a deified emperor, but the Christians mourned him as a Christian emperor who had encouraged

In the centuries following the death of Constantine, his city gradually became a Christian island in a stormy Muslim sea, and in 1493, after a 53-day siege, the great city finally fell to Sultan Mehmed II and the Ottoman Turks.

their religion, giving it stability and even grandeur. Indeed, that was Constantine's greatest achievement. By his unswerving commitment to Christianity, he left it in a position to flourish during the Dark Ages that soon followed.

Less than a century after his death, waves of Vandals and Goths broke through the frontiers of Europe, dooming the western half of the Roman Empire. As one Roman province after another fell to these tribesmen, the Roman system of organized government collapsed. Cities were deserted; communications and trade dried up, as the Dark Ages in Europe began. Constantine's well-organized, well-endowed church became a lifeline between the Romans of the west and their "barbarian" conquerors. Christian bishops, protecting their flocks, worked out arrangements with barbarian kings and their people, already half-Christianized by earlier missionaries. Christian monks, nuns, and clergy preserved the Latin language, adapting Roman laws and education to the needs of an illiterate, anarchic age. Most important of all, they brought faith and hope and comfort to their communities. Although in the ancient capital of Rome the pagan temples were looted and sacked, Constantine's great churches were untouched and remained centers of Christian pilgrimages. Rome's bishops became popes, their influence immense.

The eastern half of Constantine's empire had a different history. Within 300 years of his death, the followers of Mohammed began their tremendous sweep through the Near East and North Africa, even crossing over to Spain. Only one part of Rome's eastern empire withstood them — Constantine's impregnable capital, Constantinople, and its surrounding territories. Renamed the Byzantine Empire, it survived for another thousand years as a center of civilization and wealth, preserving not only the Christian religion within its boundaries but also much of ancient Greek and Roman culture which might otherwise have been lost.

For his profound and permanent mark on history, Constantine deserves the title that history has awarded him—Constantine the Great.

Constantine's victorious religion . . . modified the ferocious temper of the conquerors.
—EDWARD GIBBON
English historian

Further Reading

Barnes, Timothy David. *Constantine and Eusebius.* Cambridge: Harvard University Press, 1981.

———. *Early Christianity and the Roman Empire.* London: Variorum Reprints, 1984.

———. *The New Empire of Diocletian and Constantine.* Cambridge: Harvard University Press, 1982.

Bowder, Diana. *The Age of Constantine and Julian.* New York: Harper & Row, 1978.

Gibbon, Edward. *The Decline and Fall of the Roman Empire.* Abridged ed. New York: Penguin, 1983.

Harnack, Adolf von. *Militia Christi: The Christian Religion and the Military in the First Three Centuries.* Translated and introduced by David McInnes Gracie. Philadelphia: Fortress Press, 1981.

Jones, A. H. M. *Constantine and the Conversion of Europe.* London: English Universities Press, 1965.

Kee, Alistair. *Constantine Versus Christ: The Triumph of Ideology.* London: SCM Press, 1982.

Keresztes, Paul. *Constantine, A Great Christian Monarch and Apostle.* Amsterdam: J. C. Gieben, 1981.

MacMullen, Ramsey. *Constantine.* New York: Dial Press, 1969.

Neusner, Jacob. *Judaism and Christianity in the Age of Constantine: History, Messiah, Israel, and the Final Confrontation.* Chicago: University of Chicago Press, 1987.

Parker, Henry D. *Roman Legions.* Totowa, NJ: Barnes & Noble Reprints, 1971.

Russell, D. S. *From Early Judaism to Early Church.* Philadelphia: Fortress Press, 1986.

Smith, John Holland. *Constantine the Great.* New York: Scribners, 1971.

Starr, Chester G. *A History of the Ancient World.* New York: Oxford University Press, 1983.

———. *The Roman Empire: Twenty-Seven B.C. Four Hundred Seventy-Six A.D.: A Study in Survival.* New York: Oxford University Press, 1982.

Chronology

ca. 284	Born Flavius Valerius Constantine
286	Father, Constantius Chlorus, is promoted to chief military assistant and moves family to Gaul in northern Europe
293	Chlorus is named caesar of the western quarter of the Roman Empire; divorces wife Helena and marries Theodora, daughter of the emperor Maximian; Constantine is sent to live with the emperor Diocletian
303	Year of the Great Persecution (of Christians)
May 305	Abdication of Diocletian and Maximian; elevation of Chlorus to augustus, ruler of the west
July 306	Chlorus dies; Constantine is unofficially proclaimed emperor by Chlorus's troops
Oct. 312	Constantine defeats and kills Maxentius at Milvian Bridge and takes Rome
313	Proclaimed emperor of the west; Licinius becomes emperor of the east
324	Constantine defeats and kills Licinius and becomes sole emperor; work on the Christian city of Constantinople begins
May 25, 325	Constantine organizes Council of Nicaea, the first worldwide conference of Christian churches
326	Orders the death of his son Crispus and his second wife, Fausta, during a visit to Rome
327	Sends his mother, Helena, to the Holy Land as official ambassador
330	Inauguration of Constantinople
337	Constantine is baptized by the bishop of Nicomedia
May 22, 337	Dies

Index

Nancy Zinsser Walworth is a graduate of Smith College and holds an M.A. from Radcliffe College. She is coauthor of *When the World Was Rome, The World of Walls,* and *The World Awakes* and the author of *Augustus Caesar* in the Chelsea House series WORLD LEADERS—PAST & PRESENT. The mother of four and grandmother of seven, she resides with her husband in New Canaan, Connecticut.

Arthur M. Schlesinger, jr., taught history at Harvard for many years and is currently Albert Schweitzer Professor of the Humanities at City University of New York. He is the author of numerous highly praised works in American history and has twice been awarded the Pulitzer Prize. He served in the White House as special assistant to Presidents Kennedy and Johnson.

PICTURE CREDITS